Margaret Picton

Understanding Cookery

Nelson Blackie

Contents

All About Meals

Chapter

1

Why we eat

When running a home one of the most important tasks is to be able to feed your family (or merely yourself or anyone else who lives with you) well. Before you can cook varied and tasty meals you must know something about the uses of food and why it is important to our bodies. Some types of food are better for our bodies than others and you should know why. The study of foods is called **nutrition.**

Some people eat more than others but we all need a certain amount of food in order to stay alive. It is from food that our bodies get energy to do all the jobs they have to do and to keep them warm. They get the power to grow in a healthy way and to keep healthy. Without food, therefore, we would fall ill, we would have no energy to walk, dance or take part in the sports we like, and eventually our bodies would become so weak that we would die. Because food is so important and so vital to life, you must known which foods are **nutritious** so that everyone can be fed the right kinds of food to keep healthy.

Some foods are so nutritious that they help with more than one job in the body but here we have divided foods into three groups according to the main job they do:

1 Body builders;
2 Energy givers;
3 Body protectors.

1 *Body builders*

The first group of foods we will consider is the **body-building foods.** These foods help us to grow and they all contain a substance called **protein.**

There are five good body-building foods and they are the five foods which usually form the main part of any meal. They are **meat, fish, eggs, milk** and **cheese.** Let us call these the 'Top Five'.

These foods are all rich in **protein** and are excellent body-building foods. To help the 'Top Five' there is a group of vegetables which also contain protein. This group is called the **pulse** vegetables and consists of peas, beans and lentils.

Most other vegetables contain protein in small amounts. Cereals and nuts are also good body-building foods. These vegetable sources of protein are very important especially for the group of people who, for religious or health reasons, will not eat meat, eggs, milk or cheese. Do you know the name for these people? They are called **vegetarians.** Strict vegetarians can still get a good supply of protein by eating pulse vegetables, cereals and nuts but their diet cannot be as varied as a normal one. **Lacto-vegetarians** do not eat meat but they do include milk, cheese and eggs in their diet.

Here is a chart which shows all the body-building foods:

Animal protein	1 **Meat** 2 **Fish** 3 **Eggs** 4 **Milk** 5 **Cheese**	Excellent body-building foods
Vegetable protein	1 **Peas** 2 **Beans** 3 **Lentils** 4 **Nuts** 5 **Cereals**	Good sources of protein. Strict vegetarians must get all their protein from this group

Remember that all vegetables contain small amounts of protein. Potatoes contain a little but because potatoes are eaten regularly the amount of protein obtained from this group can be quite considerable, especially from new potatoes.

2 Energy givers

The second group of foods to consider is the group which supplies our bodies with energy for all the physical activities involved in staying alive and for warmth. This group consists of sugars, starches and fats.

Here is a chart showing the main foods which supply energy:

Sugars	1 **Chocolates and sweets** 2 **Cakes and pastries** 3 **Jams** 4 **Sugar** 5 **Honey** 6 **Syrup and treacle** 7 **Fresh and dried fruits**	Sugars and starches are called carbohydrates. They supply the body with most of its energy.
Starches	1 **Potatoes** 2 **Cereals** 3 **Bread** 4 **Flour and pastries**	
Fats and fatty foods	1 **Lard** 2 **Margarine** 3 **Butter** 4 **Dripping** 5 **Suet** 6 **All vegetable fats** 7 **Cod liver oil** 8 **All cooking oils** 9 **Bacon** 10 **Meat** 11 **Sausages** 12 **Fatty fish** 13 **Fried foods** 14 **Dairy produce** 15 **Nuts**	Fats and fatty foods are concentrated sources of energy.

The energy in food is measured in **kilocalories** or **kilojoules** (1 kcal = 4.19 kJ). 1 gram carbohydrate supplies the body with 4 kilocalories (16 kJ). 1 gram fat supplies the body with 9 kilocalories (38 kJ). If you eat more kilocalories than your body requires, the excess kilocalories are stored as fat. You will put on weight and become obese and this can be dangerous to your health. To reduce weight, cut down on your daily intake of fats and sugars. It is far better to get your body's energy requirements from starchy foods, such as: potatoes (rich in vitamin C and with some protein), wholemeal bread and brown rice (both containing vitamins and dietary fibre).

There is another reason for reducing the fat content in the diet. A low fat diet means less **cholesterol** in the blood. Cholesterol is a fatty substance which causes some forms of heart disease.

Some foods are low in cholesterol and are therefore a guard against heart disease, others are high in cholesterol. Look at the lists to see which ones.

Dietary fibre (sometimes referred to as **roughage**) is an indigestible form of carbohydrate which adds bulk to the diet. It should be included in meals to prevent constipation, diseases of the lower intestine, gallstones, and some types of heart disease.

Dietary fibre is found in:
1 Some breakfast cereals;
2 Fresh fruit;
3 Fresh vegetables;
4 Wholemeal bread;
5 Brown rice (i.e. still with the bran or fibrous covering).

3 Body protectors

Our last group of foods has the important job of looking after the health of our bodies. These foods contain substances called **mineral salts** and **vitamins**. Mineral salts and vitamins are found in small amounts in most foods.

There are many different mineral salts but the three most important ones are: **iron, iodine** and **calcium.** The following table shows which foods supply these mineral salts, and the parts of the body each mineral salt protects.

Foods low in cholesterol

Corn, sunflower or safflower oil;
Margarine and cooking fat made from polyunsaturated fats;
Lean cuts of meat;
Low-fat protein foods, such as chicken, veal, white fish.

Foods high in cholesterol

Eggs;
Animal fats;
Fatty meat (beef, mutton, lamb, pork, bacon, sausage);
Dairy produce;
Fatty fish (salmon, mackerel, sardine, pilchard);
Fried foods;
Home-made cakes, pastries and biscuits;
Mayonnaise.

Mineral	Where found	*Why necessary*
Iron	Liver, meat, raisins, eggs, black treacle, bread	*Iron helps to make the red colouring in blood and prevents anaemia*
Iodine	Salt, fish and tap-water	*Iodine helps to keep the thyroid gland in the neck healthy*
Calcium	Milk, cheese, eggs and green vegetables	*Calcium helps to form strong bones and teeth*

Vitamins are substances which are ***vital*** to life. They are found in tiny amounts in fresh fruits and vegetables and in dairy produce (e.g. milk, cheese, butter and eggs). Vitamins are named after letters of the alphabet and the most important ones are vitamins A, B, C and D. The table shows where these are found and why they are important to our bodies.

Vitamins	Where found	*Why necessary*
A	Animal fats, margarine, cod liver oil, milk, cheese and red vegetables (e.g. carrots)	*Vitamin A helps to keep the eyes healthy*
B	Bread, liver, egg-yolk, milk, marmite, yeast, and the germs of cereals	*Vitamin B helps to keep the nervous system healthy*
C	Citrus fruits, green vegetables, tomatoes, rose-hip syrup, blackcurrants	*Vitamin C helps to keep the skin healthy*
D	Animal fats, cod liver oil, milk, cheese, oily fish	*Vitamin D helps to keep the bones healthy*

A diet which is short of vitamins causes ***deficiency diseases.*** For example, people living in the Asiatic countries (such as India, China and Korea) who live on a diet consisting chiefly of rice (starch) suffer from many of these diseases. Their diet does not contain the variety of foods which supply us with vitamins. Can you remember which these foods are? A shortage of these foods causes the diseases listed alongside.

Vitamin shortage	Disease
A	Night blindness, an eye disease
B	Beri-beri and pellagra, diseases of the nerves
C	Scurvy, a skin disease
D	Rickets, a bone disease

These deficiency diseases are not very common in Britain where a normally varied diet has adequate amounts of the vitamins required by the body.

Water also helps to keep the body healthy. It is present in nearly all foods and is responsible for cleansing the body.

Can you see now why it is so important to learn about nutrition? In the next chapter we will use this knowledge when we learn how to plan balanced meals but before we do this let us summarize the main points so far. Food is essential to us. Eating is necessary for growth, energy and good health. It can also be a very pleasant pastime. To remind you of the food groups here is a simple chart:

Nutrient	Function
1 *Protein*	Growth; body-building
2 *Fats* *Sugars* *Starches*	Energy for work and heat
3 *Mineral salts* *Vitamins*	Protection from disease

Think and Do

1. Collect pictures of foods from magazines and stick them into your scrap book. At the side of each picture print: *a.* the food value of the foods in the picture; *b.* what the foods do for the body.

2. Make a list of as many sugars and starches as you can think of which begin with the letters 'S' and 'P'.

3. An anagram is a word which can be formed by re-arranging a group of letters. Solve the following anagrams. They are all well-known foods.

Body-building foods: ESEHCE; ETMA; GSEG; IKLM; UTNS.

Energy-giving foods: DARBE; ALDR; NEOYH; SETTPAOO; STEU; RECI; TURETB; RAEGRIMAN; ILO; GSURA.

Body-protecting foods: GONSRAE; TETUCLE; BSESURLS SOTPSRU; RTGIPEUARF; ETOSAMTO; RROASTC.

4. Are these sentences **true** or **false?**

a. Oranges are rich in vitamin C.

b. Bananas supply the body with energy.

c. Sugars and starches are two groups of carbohydrates.

d. Meat is a protein food and is therefore body-building.

e. Margarine contains vitamins A and D.

f. Foods containing iron help to prevent anaemia.

g. Sugar is a body-protector.

h. Potatoes contain starch which gives energy.

i. Water helps to keep us warm.

j. Mineral salts and vitamins are found in fresh fruits and vegetables.

5. In what way does each of these foods help our bodies?

a. bread, brussels sprouts, bacon, beetroot.

b. carrots, cheese, cornflakes, cod liver oil.

c. liver, lettuce, lard, luncheon meat.

d. marmalade, meat, margarine, milk.

6. Plan a day's meal for a strict vegetarian. Remember to include a good supply of protein.

7. The following are snack meals. Copy the meals into your notebook and underline the body-building foods in red, and the body-protecting foods in green.

a. Cheese on toast with tomato. An apple. A glass of milk.

b. Baked beans on toast with a poached egg. Orange juice.

c. Mushroom omelette with bread and butter. A cup of coffee.

d. Fish fingers with parsley sauce and chipped potatoes. Sliced banana with ice cream. A cup of tea.

8. Find out about the following and write a few sentences in your books about each of them.

a. Anaemia.

b. Dietary fibre.

c. Cholesterol.

9. Complete the crossword shown.

10. Design a poster which you think would guide people to buy the right foods for good health.

Clues across

1. These vegetables supply protein

2. An excellent source of vitamin C

3. A mineral salt required to keep the blood healthy

Clues down

4. The bone disease caused by a shortage of vitamin D

5. Gives us energy

Chapter 2

Planning meals

We have discovered in the first chapter how important food is for our bodies, we must now find out how to use this knowledge in planning good and varied meals. You must think of many points before deciding which foods to buy for the day's meals. Here are five important points to consider when planning meals:

1 Every meal should be tasty and nutritious. This means that it must contain all the various nutrients required by our bodies. This type of meal is called a **balanced** meal. A balanced meal therefore contains at least one food from each of the food groups (proteins, carbohydrates, fats, mineral salts and vitamins). However simple the meal is it should still be a balanced one.

2 The **season** of the year is also important. Can you guess why? Obviously the weather must influence your choice of which dishes to prepare. You are not going to be very popular if you prepare salads on cold days in the middle of winter and stews on hot days in summer. Meals must be sensible for the time of year. You must also remember that if you can use foods which are plentiful they will be cheaper than when you try to buy them out of season. For example, a strawberry flan would be more economical to make in summer than in winter. When the weather is cold our bodies need more fats and carbohydrates than when the weather is hot. On hot summer days the amount of protective foods (i.e. fruits and vegetables) in the diet, should be increased.

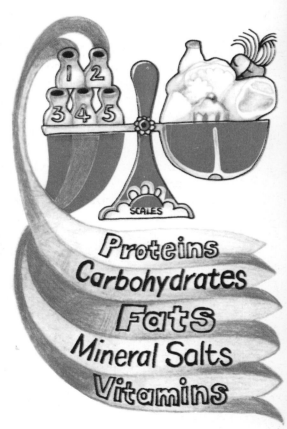

Proteins
Carbohydrates
Fats
Mineral Salts
Vitamins

3 The **age** and **occupation** of the people you are cooking for must be considered because although everybody requires some foods from each food group, the amount required will vary. For example, people doing energetic or manual jobs all day long (such as miners, steelworkers, labourers) will need a greater supply of carbohydrates (i.e. energy-giving food) than people whose jobs are not so energetic. Some simple rules to remember here are:

a A person who perspires heavily during the day (e.g. a stoker in a ship's engine room or a blast furnace worker) must have plenty of salt in his food to replace the salt he has lost through sweating.

b Growing children need plenty of protein or body-building foods and a supply of calcium to form strong teeth and bones.

c Teenagers also need plenty of protein because they are still growing. It is at this stage that skin blemishes (such as spots and pimples) can be such a nuisance. Plenty of fresh fruit and vegetables will help to keep the skin fresh and clear. Teenagers also need plenty of carbohydrates to give them energy.

d Adults need fewer carbohydrates in their diet than children but they must have a good supply of protein, for even when a person has stopped growing he or she still needs protein to repair and replace body tissues.

e Expectant mothers need a good supply of calcium in their diet so that their babies' teeth and bones will develop properly.

4 We all have some **favourite foods** and others which we do not like as much. When planning meals for other people remember the foods they enjoy and try to avoid their dislikes, although you may wish to introduce new and interesting dishes from time to time.

5 All meals should look **attractive** and **appetising.** A colourful meal looks far more inviting than a drab and colourless one. Just a little extra thought can make even the simplest of meals look attractive. A sprig of parsley or a slice of tomato gives savoury dishes extra colour and appeal. Glacé cherries, chocolate buttons and chopped nuts can be used to decorate sweet dishes. This is called garnishing a dish. Can you think of any other ways of garnishing savoury and sweet dishes? Here are two meals. Which sounds the tastier and more attractive?

a
steamed plaice
creamed potatoes
cauliflower
parsley sauce
rice pudding

b
baked plaice
chipped potatoes
peas
parsley sauce
bilberry tart, custard

Do you agree that menu *a* is too pale and insipid whereas menu *b* is more colourful? The second meal also has a variety of textures. This means that it has some dishes which are crisp to eat and some which are softer and creamier. This also helps to give a meal more interest both to the eye and to the tongue. It is useful to remember that a colourful meal is nearly always a well-balanced one.

Pastry leaves

Gherkin flower

Water lily tomato

Now let us consider the different types of meals that can be served during the day. Usually the time of day will influence the type of meal to be prepared but the working hours of members of the household will have to be considered. A shift worker will require his or her meals at home to fit in with his or her day's routine. Normally dinner is served between twelve and one o'clock but if all the members of a household are out at work or school during the day it may suit everybody to have a snack lunch at midday and then a cooked meal or dinner at home in the evening. It is necessary therefore for the members of a household to have a meal time-table to suit their own particular needs. Usually the day's meals will follow one of these patterns:

Time	Group A	Group B	Group C
7–9 a.m.	Breakfast	Breakfast	Breakfast
12–1 p.m.	Dinner	Snack lunch	Dinner
5–7 p.m.	High tea	Dinner	Snack tea
9–10 p.m.	Snack supper	Hot drink	Cooked supper

These main meals of the day are very important because if satisfying meals can be produced at the right times it will discourage the habit of eating between meals which only leads to over-weight.

CHOCS

Breakfast

This, the first meal of the day, is often considered to be the most important. Here are some points to remember when planning breakfast meals:

1 The meal must be easy and quick to prepare. Some dishes

(e.g. grapefruit) may be prepared the evening before and this will save precious time. The table can also be laid in the evening.

2 The meal should be substantial as it will normally be the only food eaten before midday. It must not, however, be a heavy meal because it is difficult to digest rich and heavy foods first thing in the morning. However simple the meal is, it should contain at least one protein food and a hot drink.

3 It is always wise to start the day with something nourishing as it may have to last the person until dinner-time as he or she may not have time for much of a snack at lunch-time. On those terrible mornings when the alarm fails to go off and everyone sleeps in and is late in getting up, a simple snack is far better than nothing at all and even a hurried bite can still be nutritious. Here are some suggestions for nutritious snacks for the late sleeper:

a A slice of cheese and a cup of tea.
b A dripping or bacon sandwich and a hot drink.
c A slice of toast with marmite and a hot drink.
d Fresh fruit, a biscuit and a glass of hot milk.

It is not wise to go without breakfast too often.

For those of you who get up in good time to have breakfast, the meal can be as exciting as any other. Here are some suggestions:

Start off with something refreshing, e.g.

Fruit juice	Tomato juice
Stewed fruit	Melon
Grapefruit or orange	Porridge (on cold days)
Cereal	Yoghurt

Follow with one of these cooked dishes, e.g.

Fried bacon and egg	Grilled kippers
Bacon with baked beans	Omelette
Scrambled egg on toast	Smoked haddock and poached egg
Welsh rarebit	Grilled mushrooms, tomato and
Pilchards on toast	bacon
Poached egg on toast	Fried sausage with apple rings and tomato

Finish with toast and marmalade and a hot drink.

These are just a few of the many breakfast dishes that are suitable. Can you suggest a few others?

Dinner or Lunch

You can really show your skill in preparing varied and unusual dishes when it comes to the main meal of the day. Dinner or lunch should consist of at least two courses but three is usual.

1 Appetizer. This can be selected from the following: soup, grapefruit, fruit juice, fresh fruit, hors d'œuvres (a selection of savoury foods such as pilchards, sliced tomatoes, gherkins, shrimps, olives, etc.).

2 The Savoury Course. This should have a body-building food, at least two vegetables and any accompanying sauces and gravies. The more unusual vegetables are often neglected but they can make a very welcome change from the normal choice of carrots, cabbage and peas. When you next visit a large greengrocery have a look at the variety of vegetables and try to plan meals using them as alternatives to the vegetables you normally have. Look out for chicory, endive, aubergine, broccoli, spinach, globe and Jerusalem artichokes, peppers, marrows, leeks, asparagus and corn on the cob.

3 The Sweet Course. This can be cold or hot, depending on the weather but it should contrast in colour and texture to the savoury course of the meal.

Here are a variety of balanced meals suitable for dinner or lunch. Try to cook some of them in your assignment work at school or at home during the weekends. If you have not heard of these dishes, look them up in the index of your recipe book and see how they are prepared.

1 Toad-in-the-hole, creamed potatoes, cabbage, gravy. Fruit sponge, custard.

2 Liver and bacon casserole, jacket potatoes, brussels sprouts. Apple dumplings, custard.

3 Grilled pork chops, apple sauce, roasted potatoes, stuffed tomatoes, peas, gravy. Jam layer pudding, white sauce.

4 Russian fish pie, chipped potatoes, beetroot in white sauce. Fruit fool.

5 Mixed grill, baked potatoes, cauliflower, cheese sauce. Bakewell tart, custard.

6 Cheese and potato pie, beans, white sauce. Blackberry crumble, custard.

7 Brown stew with dumplings, jacket potatoes, broccoli. Queen of puddings.

8 Curried eggs, rice, peas. Stewed damsons, custard.

9 Shepherd's pie, asparagus, gravy. Raspberry flan, cream.

10 Roast beef, Yorkshire pudding, roast potatoes, leeks, gravy. Rice pudding, sliced banana.

High Tea

High tea is a lighter meal than dinner or lunch. It usually consists of a savoury dish which may be served with potatoes and another vegetable, or with bread and butter; a cold sweet and followed with a drink. Here are some ideas for high teas:

1 Grilled fish cakes, sliced tomatoes, bread and butter. Fruit in jelly, cakes.

2 Cornish pasties, chipped potatoes, green salad. Blancmange.

3 Scotch eggs, continental salad, bread and butter. Apple pie, cream.

4 Spaghetti à la Bolognaise, grated cheese. Chocolate mousse, fresh fruit.

5 Soused herrings, green salad, bread and butter. Fresh fruit.

6 Bacon and egg pie, chipped potatoes, grated raw carrot. Trifle, cakes.

7 Baked cheese potatoes, tomato sauce, corn on the cob. Apple fritters.

8 Grilled beefburgers, chipped potatoes, peas. Egg custard tart.

9 Baked stuffed plaice, parsley sauce, broad beans. Manchester tart, fresh fruit.

10 Cold cooked meat, green salad, bread and butter. Caramel custard, cakes.

In Scotland and some parts of England, high tea is more elaborate. Instead of a sweet course there is a large selection of home-made bread, cakes, biscuits and scones on the table. The meal is rounded off with a drink of tea. Here is a typical Scottish high tea:

Fried sausages, mashed potatoes, baked beans. Oatcake with butter and cheese. Fruit scones. Assorted home-made biscuits. Toasted crumpets and bread rolls. Home-made cakes.

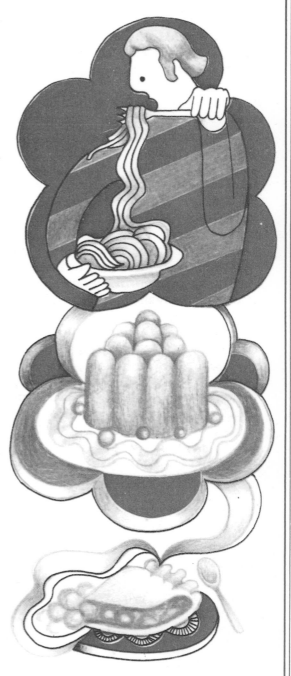

Suppers

Supper snacks can be a problem. They need to be tasty and nutritious but also easy to eat because one eye may be fastened on the television while eating or drinking. Here are a few ideas:

cauliflower au gratin; grilled kipper fillets on toast; toasted savoury sandwiches; sausage or pilchard rolls with pickles; savoury pasties; cheese Scotch eggs; grilled fish fingers; soup with toast; hot dogs; pizzas.

Convenience foods

Busy people are glad to get as much help as possible in preparing tasty meals. It can be a lengthy job but today's range of convenience foods such as packet mixes, tinned and frozen foods can all help to save time and energy in the kitchen. The convenience food when prepared can become part of a whole meal, as shown in the following examples, rather than being served on its own:

1 Frozen cod steaks, cheese sauce, new potatoes, peas. Tinned oranges, cream.

2 Tinned baked beans, poached egg, grilled bacon. Packet orange meringue pie.

3 Packet prawn curry, rice. Fresh fruit, ice-cream.

4 Frozen chicken casserole, baked potatoes, stuffed marrow. Pancakes from packet mix.

These convenience foods are a modern aid and a valuable help if wisely used. In the next chapter we shall discuss more of the modern trends in buying food and learn also how to budget and cost our meals.

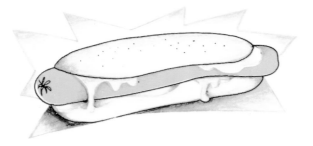

Think and Do

1. Copy out the following diagram into your books.

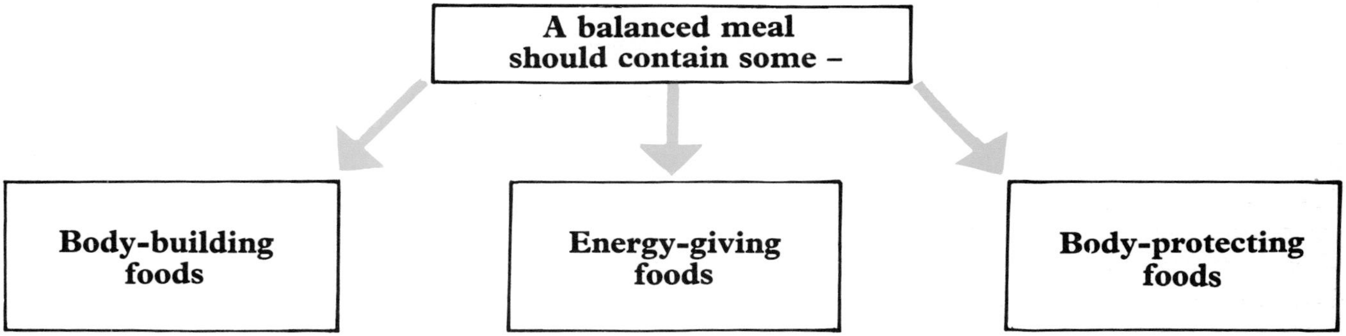

```
          ┌─────────────────────────┐
          │    A balanced meal      │
          │  should contain some –  │
          └─────────────────────────┘
```

| Body-building foods | Energy-giving foods | Body-protecting foods |

2. Check each of these meals and say whether or not they are balanced:

a. Roast beef, Yorkshire pudding, creamed potatoes, carrots, gravy. Rice pudding.

b. Sausages, mashed potatoes. Steamed pudding, jam sauce.

c. Cornish pasties, chipped potatoes, peas. Stewed apple, custard.

d. Fish cakes, baked potatoes, parsley sauce. Lemon meringue pie.

e. Macaroni and cheese pie, brussels sprouts. Apple dumplings, custard.

3. Complete the following so that they give balanced meals:

a. Baked liver, ..., ..., ..., ..., custard.

b. Russian fish pie, parsley sauce, ..., ...

c. ...., ..., carrots, gravy. Apple crumble, ...

d. Scotch eggs, ..., ... Fruit flan, ...

4. Suggest a suitable sweet dish for each of the following meals. Remember that a contrast in colour and texture adds appeal.

a. Brown stew, boiled potatoes, carrots.

b. Meat and potato pie, carrots, gravy.

c. Grilled steak, stuffed tomatoes, peas, gravy.

d. Soused herrings, new potatoes, green salad, salad dressing.

e. Shepherd's pie, spring cabbage, gravy.

5. Plan suitable balanced meals for the following occasions:

a. a lunch for a mother with a young baby.

b. a high tea for two shorthand typists.

c. a dinner for a miner returning from work.

d. breakfast for two old age pensioners.

e. Sunday dinner for a family on a cold winter's day.

f. a high tea for two schoolgirls after a hockey match.

g. a summer breakfast.

h. a high tea in Glasgow.

6. Solve the following anagrams which, when completed, will give you a mixed grill:

PEHPCID OTEOTPAS; AGEUSSSA; ILTEFL ETSKA; TEMOSTAO; KENIYD; LERIV; FERID INNSOO; RSUOHMOSM.

7. Suggest ways of garnishing the following dishes:

a. fish cakes; *b.* lemon mousse; *c.* cheese soufflé; *d.* bread and butter pudding; *e.* Victoria sandwich; *f.* Quiche Lorraine; *g.* brown stew; *h.* hot pot; *i.* boiled new potatoes; *j.* pancakes; *k.* tuna pizza; *l.* jacket potatoes; *m.* meat loaf.

8. The following hors d'œuvres are served at a dinner. Can you name each item?

UEMBCCUR; TUSN; RETOEBTO; IHASRD; VSOILE; HSLAICRPD; PWSRAN; SOTMATOE.

9. List as many different ways of cooking potatoes as you can think of.

10. When you next visit your greengrocer's find out the prices of the following unusual vegetables:

a. two aubergines; *b.* 500 g spinach; *c.* 1 medium-sized marrow; *d.* a bunch of asparagus; *e.* 500 g green peppers; *f.* 2 globe artichokes; *g.* ½ kilo broccoli; *h.* a sweet corn cob.

Chapter 3

Planning the shopping

On a shopping trip food can be purchased from many different types of shops. You may choose to shop at the large and modern supermarket with its wide range of pre-packed foods, or you may prefer the smaller shop where you can get personal attention.

Big versus small

Let us first look at the advantages and disadvantages of shopping at a supermarket. Supermarkets are modern shops and they have up-to-date coverings on walls, floors and ceilings, making them hygienic as well as attractive. There are rows and rows of shelves on which the food is displayed, and you can walk round the shop at your leisure, selecting your goods. A wide choice is always available, and most foods are hygienically packed in cellophane wrapping. Supermarkets sell a large variety of items ranging from groceries, greengroceries and meat to dairy produce, confectionery, medicines and household goods. It is possible, therefore, for you sometimes to do all your shopping in the same shop and this can save time and energy. Bargain offers can help to save a few pennies, here and there, and most supermarkets have bargain offers each week. You can see why many people like to shop at the supermarket.

There are, however, some disadvantages to this type of shopping. Let us consider them. Many shoppers are confused by the large variety of goods which are on display and sometimes buy more than they had intended. The music, which is sometimes played in supermarkets, can divert the attention of the shopper and this might lead to unwise purchases. People who like the personal attention of shop assistants find supermarkets to be unfriendly places. Some dislike having to walk around the shop, particularly in the very large supermarkets, because this can be tiring when there are other chores waiting to be done. Sometimes large queues form at the cashier's till and all the time saved by shopping under the one roof can be lost waiting to pay for the purchases. Mistakes can be made at the check-out where busy assistants wrongly charge for some items and it is not easy to notice the accidental errors as the prices are registered at the till. There is often no delivery service and the groceries have all to be carried home unless one can load them into a car.

Many people feel the advantages of supermarket shopping outweigh the disadvantages but you must decide for yourself.

We have looked at the supermarkets; let us examine the advantages and disadvantages of the small shops.

Assistants in the small shop can provide the individual attention and the courtesy and friendliness which is sometimes missing in the supermarkets. The assistant often knows the likes and dislikes of the local family and can recommend items to suit their tastes. Orders may be delivered, for a small charge, often after being telephoned, and arrangements can be made with the shopkeeper to pay weekly or monthly for goods purchased. This type of shopping is best for anyone who likes personal service and attention.

Shopping at the smaller shops has its disadvantages also. There is not as wide a variety of goods as at the supermarket, and smaller shops cannot afford to have as many bargain offers. Customers often have to wait a long time before it is their turn to be served, and in order to get served quickly, unsuitable purchases can be made.

When is a bargain not a bargain?

Bargain offers can be very tempting but are they always bargains? Next time you see an offer in a shop window which you would like to buy, stop and think. Ask yourself these four questions:

FOR

1. Wide choice of foods available
2. Hygienic surroundings
3. Bright, cheery atmosphere
4. Bargain offers
5. All types of commodities sold

AGAINST

1. May spend too much money
2. Can be tiring walking around
3. No personal attention
4. Difficult to check prices at till
5. May have to queue to pay for goods

1. Will I be able to use it?
2. Do I need it?
3. Would I have bought it if it had not been on offer?
4. Is it really cheaper?

If you can answer **yes** to three or all of these questions, then the offer might well be worth buying. But do remember to check that the price reduction is correct. Look for the weight and see that this has not been reduced as well as the price.

Buying food wisely

Try to plan a few meals in advance and then you can easily work out a shopping list of all the items you will need. The grocery order of butter, tea, sugar, etc., will probably not vary from week to week, and this could be a regular weekly order delivered by your grocer. Extra groceries needed, e.g. sauces, dried fruit, should be jotted down so that you do not forget them. Meat, fish, greengroceries and dairy produce, such as milk, eggs, and cheese, should be bought as they are required and not stored for any length of time. It helps, when shopping, to have a shopping list handy with the items listed in groups according to the shops at which you expect to buy them.

Here are a few tips to help you with your shopping:

1. Groceries are cheaper if they are bought in bulk or in large quantities. Check, however, that you have enough storage space at home.

2. Greengroceries can be expensive. Always buy fruits which are in season and plentiful, because they will then be cheap. Do not forget that the cheaper vegetables (e.g. carrots, cabbage) are equally as nutritious as the dearer vegetables (e.g. cauliflower, brussels sprouts).

3. When buying fish, shop economically. If you are going to make a fish pie or fish cakes, where the flavour of the fish will be hidden, choose the cheapest white fish. Whiting is as nutritious as plaice, haddock or cod. Curing or freezing does not affect food value so smoked or frozen fish can also be used. Herrings are very rich in food value relative to their cost. Try them grilled or soused and served with salad for tea or supper.

4. When buying meat, select a suitable cut for the dish you

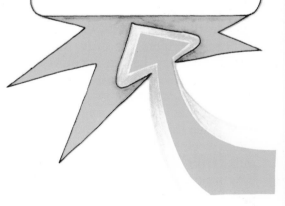

Shopping List

Greengrocer

1 kg carrots
1 spring cabbage
2 kg potatoes

Grocer

500g currants
1 medium salad cream
1 pkt fish dressing

Butcher

500g streaky bacon
500g minced meat

Fishmonger

4 fillets of plaice

have in mind. The butcher will always offer advice if you are uncertain which cut to ask for. For stews, casseroles, puddings, pies and curries, choose cheap cuts of meat. For roasts and grills, choose dearer cuts of meat. If the housekeeping money is running short and you would like a cheap joint of meat try brisket of beef or breast of lamb or a joint from the spare rib of pork.

Budgeting

When budgeting the housekeeping be sensible and make sure that you are not left with outstanding bills at the end of the week. How much money should be spent on food each week? This, of course, will vary considerably from family to family or household to household. It will depend on the number of people, their appetites, and the money coming into the house (income). As a rough guide approximately one third of the weekly income should be spent on food. Many households will spend more than that and many will spend less.

Imagine a family group of Mother, Father and 1 teenager at school with a combined family income of £120 per week. One third of this is £40 which the family can be expected to spend on food each week. The teenager will be having a midday snack at school (at a reasonable cost) so this family should manage on this figure.

Imagine another group of Mother, Father and 3 children, only one of whom is at school so the mother cannot go out to work. The income is £90 of which one third would be £30 for spending on food. This might not be enough for 5 people when only one child will be getting a midday snack at school but, on the other hand, younger children may eat less.

These budgets are only for food purposes. If the housekeeping money has to account for cleaning materials, newspapers, stationery and postage stamps, children's pocket money, etc., then more money will have to be allowed.

Once the housekeeping money has been allocated it is a good idea to keep it separately from any personal money. Each week you will have to pay for meat or fish, groceries, milk, fruit and vegetables, and bread. It is impossible to say how much should be spent on each of these items because it will differ from household to household, but here are some important points that you should remember when budgeting:

1 Allow for 500 ml of milk per person per day.
2 Allow for 2 good helpings of meat, fish, eggs or cheese per person per day.
3 Allow for 1 good helping of green vegetables per person per day.
4 Allow for some fresh fruit per person per day.
5 Allow for 1 helping of potatoes and 1 helping of bread or cereals per person per day.

When you have allowed enough money to cover these essential items, the rest of the housekeeping money can be spent on foods to suit your family's likes and appetites.

Think and Do

1. Name four cheap cuts of meat and suggest four dishes for which they could be used.

2. Visit your local supermarket and jot down what you like and what you dislike about shopping there. Write this into your notebooks in the form of an essay under the heading 'The Local Supermarket'.

3. To help you to work out the cost of meals prepare a price chart in your books. Draw two columns and label them COMMODITY and PRICE. Under the heading COMMODITY write as many foods as you can think of. Find out the current price of each item and write this in the PRICE column.

4. The Jones family consists of Mother, Father and 2 children aged 14 years and 10 years. The weekly income is £180. How much money do you think they will spend on food each week? Work out how much milk they will need during the week and the cost of their weekly milk bill.

5. Ask at home if you can help to budget the week's housekeeping. In doing this, prepare the weekly shopping list for groceries and ask if you can be responsible for the shopping.

6. Write a poem about a local shopkeeper or supermarket.

7. What are the advantages and disadvantages of buying groceries in bulk?

8. Complete the following crossword.

Clues across
1. A white fish
2. An economical joint of pork
3. A cheap joint of beef

Clues down
1. A nutritious but cheap vegetable
4. The money coming into a family
5. It will help to make this before going shopping

Chapter

4

Laying tables and entertaining guests

Laying the table at mealtimes is a simple task that most of you do regularly at home. I wonder how many of you find this an unwelcome chore that is done as quickly as possible. In this chapter we shall learn how to lay tables correctly and how to make them look attractive and exciting as well.

Choosing the correct cutlery

Can you recognize all the different kinds of knives, forks and spoons? Here to help you is a series of diagrams. Each piece of cutlery is labelled with its name and the course of a meal for which it is used.

This is a Tablespoon

Never used for eating but can be used for serving dishes

This is a Teaspoon

It is used when eating grapefruit and for stirring drinks

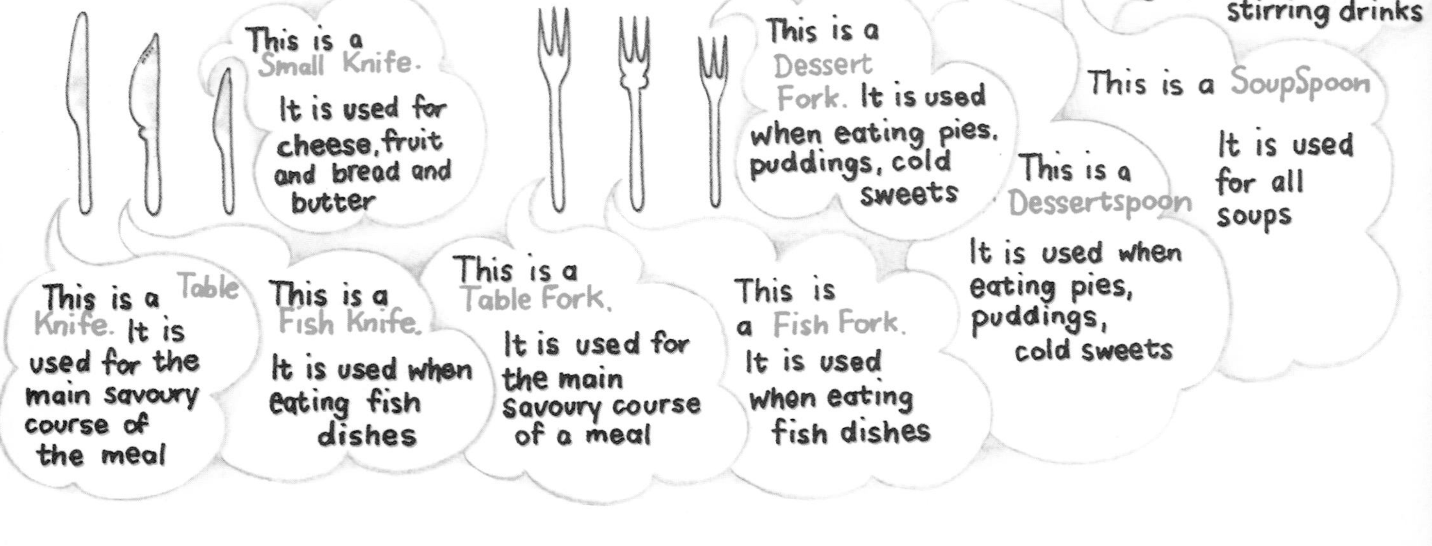

This is a Small Knife. It is used for cheese, fruit and bread and butter

This is a Dessert Fork. It is used when eating pies, puddings, cold sweets

This is a SoupSpoon

It is used for all soups

This is a Dessertspoon

It is used when eating pies, puddings, cold sweets

This is a Table Knife. It is used for the main savoury course of the meal

This is a Fish Knife. It is used when eating fish dishes

This is a Table Fork. It is used for the main savoury course of a meal

This is a Fish Fork. It is used when eating fish dishes

Always lay tables with the correct cutlery for the meal being served. Here are diagrams of place settings for three different meals of the day. Would you have chosen the cutlery illustrated?

1 A breakfast meal consisting of fried bacon, egg and tomato; marmalade and toast; coffee.

2 A dinner consisting of chicken soup; roast beef and Yorkshire pudding, spring cabbage, roast potatoes, gravy; Bakewell tart and custard.

3 A high tea consisting of Russian fish pie, salad, bread and butter; fruit flan, cream; cherry cake.

Points to remember when laying place settings

1 Allow enough room in between the cutlery to be able to put the plate down easily.

2 Check that all knife blades face **inwards.**

3 Place the dessert spoon **above** the dessert fork.

4 Lay the cutlery in the correct order. This means that the cutlery, for the first course, should be on the outside, the cutlery for the second course should be in towards the middle, and so on.

When you go out to dinner you may be confused by all the different knives, forks and spoons before you, and the place setting may look very different from the type you are used to at home. Keep calm. Pick up the cutlery on the outside and then work inwards for each following course and you will find that you have used the correct cutlery for each dish. Below is an example of a place setting that you may come across at weddings, dinner dances and other similar special occasion meals.

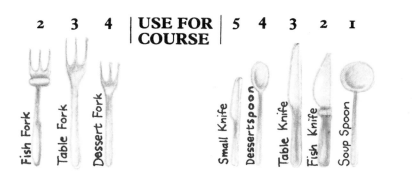

				USE FOR					
2	3	4		COURSE	5	4	3	2	1
Fish Fork	Table Fork	Dessert Fork			Small Knife	Dessertspoon	Table Knife	Fish Knife	Soup Spoon

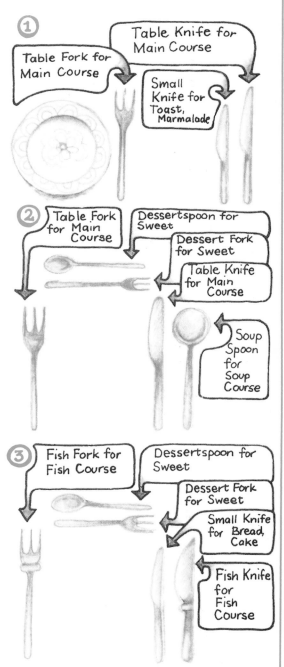

① Table Fork for Main Course — Table Knife for Main Course — Small Knife for Toast, Marmalade

② Table Fork for Main Course — Dessertspoon for Sweet — Dessert Fork for Sweet — Table Knife for Main Course — Soup Spoon for Soup Course

③ Fish Fork for Fish Course — Dessertspoon for Sweet — Dessert Fork for Sweet — Small Knife for Bread, Cake — Fish Knife for Fish Course

Articles for the table

Now that we have learned the correct cutlery to use when laying tables, let us consider the other articles we shall need for the table.

1 Table covering. If a meal is being served in the kitchen on a formica-covered table, then no further covering is needed. This type of surface cannot be burned by hot dishes or be scratched by cutlery. It is easy to keep clean because a quick wipe with a damp cloth will remove most stains.

If a meal is being served on an attractive wooden-topped table, then individual place mats can be used. These can be made of plastic, formica or cork and need only be wiped with a damp cloth after being used. Some place mats are woven from grasses and look very attractive on a polished table top. This type needs shaking well after use and the occasional wipe with a damp cloth. Cotten and linen place mats have to be washed like tablecloths, but they look lovely when they have been crisply starched.

If a tablecloth is being used it should be gay and practical. Where there are small children a plastic tablecloth is quite suitable, or a seersucker cotton or nylon cloth which can be easily washed and drip-dried. Whatever type of cloth you choose, check that it is **clean** before laying the table.

2 Water glasses and jugs. All glassware on a table should be sparkling clean. A final polish with a dry tea towel as the table is being laid, will make glassware look far better.

3 Salt and pepper sets (Condiment sets). Always check when laying a table that the salt and pepper pots are full.

4 Heat-proof mats. Heat-proof mats should be put at each place-setting and down the middle of the table, in readiness for the hot serving dishes. These will not be needed if a formica-topped table is being used.

5 Serving cutlery. When dishes are to be served at the table, special cutlery should be provided. Tablespoons can be used for most dishes though a knife will be required for any dish that needs cutting, e.g. a pie or flan.

6 Serviettes. It is always a good idea to use a serviette at mealtimes. It will protect your clothes and stop crumbs from falling onto the floor. Paper serviettes or napkins made

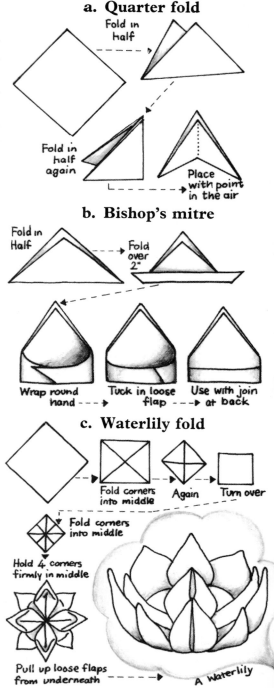

a. Quarter fold
Fold in half
Fold in half again
Place with point in the air

b. Bishop's mitre
Fold in Half
Fold over 2"
Wrap round hand
Tuck in loose flap
Use with join at back

c. Waterlily fold
Fold corners into middle
Again
Turn over
Fold corners into middle
Hold 4 corners firmly in middle
Pull up loose flaps from underneath
A Waterlily

from material can be used. There are many simple ways of folding napkins to make them look more exciting. Do try some of these simple folds. You will be surprised how attractive a table can look when the serviettes are neatly arranged.

7 Decoration. A table always looks more attractive if a small decoration is added. Flowers will give colour and freshness at any time of the year. When flowers are too expensive, use twigs or sprigs of evergreen. Pine cones, when they have been washed, can be used to make a delightful table decoration. A bowl of fruit will add a splash of colour and there might be room on the table for an attractive ornament. If you are giving a special dinner party you may wish to use candles. A meal by candlelight has extra appeal. When you are making a table decoration, remember to keep it **small** and **low**. Tall, floral arrangements may look delightful but they are not very practical at a table.

Here are some simple table decorations which you might like to make for yourselves.

For special occasion meals a decorative *menu card* will add interest to the table.

A flower head floating in a wine glass or low glass

Twigs used with pine cones

A cluster of small flowers in a gravy boat

A bowl of fruit decorated with holly or ivy leaves

A candle decorated with holly leaves

A piece of driftwood or bark with a hole cut in the middle and flowers arranged in the hole

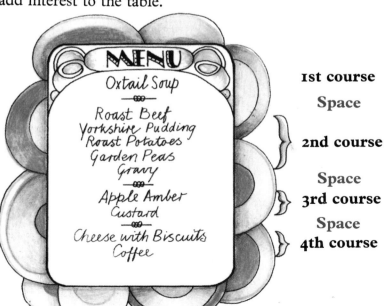

MENU

Oxtail Soup

Roast Beef
Yorkshire Pudding
Roast Potatoes
Garden Peas
Gravy

Apple Amber
Custard

Cheese with Biscuits
Coffee

1st course

Space

2nd course

Space
3rd course

Space
4th course

Menus

A menu is a list of all the dishes in a meal. In restaurants a menu will give a choice of dishes for each course of the meal, and the diner will order from the choice given.

A 'home-made' menu card should always be neatly written with the dishes arranged underneath each other. All the dishes in one course should be grouped together and a space should be left between each different course. The main item of each course should be at the top with any accompaniments underneath. On page 27 is an example of how a menu should be written.

Try to think of some unusual shapes for home-made menu cards. The ones shown here will give you some ideas.

A restaurant menu often looks complicated at first glance but the following points will help you to understand it. There are two types of menu—*Table d'hôte* and *A la carte.*

A table d'hôte menu consists of a suggested complete meal. There will be a choice of two or three dishes in each course but the choice is usually limited. There is one fixed price for the complete meal and this will be printed at the top of the menu.

An *à la carte* menu is longer than a table d'hôte one, but it gives you a greater variety of choice of dishes. You can have as many courses as you like, and each dish has its own price on the menu.

On the opposite page are two menus—one is table d'hôte and the other is à la carte. Choose a meal from each menu and work out the price you would have to pay in a restaurant.

Cut out menu cards in special shapes. At Christmas, try them in the shape of a tree, sprig of holly or Father Christmas

A coloured card fan with a lacy d'oyley and printed menu in the middle

Cut menu card in the shape of a scroll

Design individual cards with guests own initial painted on.

Use an old birthday or Christmas card and stick the menu over the verse

Cut out silhouette shapes from old cards and mount them on white paper. Print the menu opposite

TABLE D'HÔTE £1.50

Fruit juice
Tomato soup
Grapefruit cocktail

Roast lamb and mint sauce
Roast pork and apple sauce
Grilled sausage and bacon
Fried haddock and tartare sauce
Roast potatoes, Chipped potatoes
Peas, Carrots, Cabbage

Steamed jam sponge and custard
Rice pudding
Trifle
Cheese and biscuits

A LA CARTE

Melon with ginger   60p
Prawn cocktail   70p
Celery soup   24p
Chilled grapefruit   40p
Hors d'œuvres   60p

Fried plaice with tartare sauce   £1.40
Scampi with tartare sauce   £1.80
Roast turkey with stuffing   £1.50
Pork chops with apple sauce   £1.40
Veal and ham pie   £1.20
Salmon salad   £1.20
Chicken Maryland   £1.80

Creamed potatoes   24p
New potatoes   30p
Roast potatoes   24p
Croquette potatoes   24p
Garden peas   20p
Sweet corn   20p
Cauliflower   20p
Mushrooms   20p
Tomatoes   20p
Broccoli   20p

Caramel custard   40p
Apple pie and custard   40p
Sherry trifle   50p
Coffee soufflé   50p
Crêpes Suzette   50p
Fruit flan   40p

Black coffee   24p (with cream 30p)

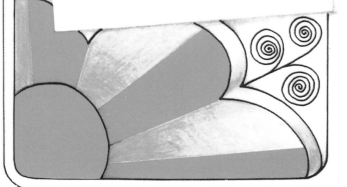

Many restaurants have menus which are written in French. Here are some common French terms which you will find useful to learn.

agneau	lamb	**jus**	fruit juice
ananas	pineapple	**légumes**	vegetables
au gratin	covered with breadcrumbs or cheese sauce and browned in the oven	**mornay**	coated with a cheese sauce
beignets	fritters	**mouton**	mutton
bœuf	beef	**œufs**	eggs
café	coffee	**pêches**	peaches
canard	duck	**pois**	peas
carottes	carrots	**poisson**	fish
champignons	mushrooms	**pommes**	apples
consommé	clear soup	**pommes de terre**	potatoes
coupe Jacques	fruit topped with ice cream and cream	**potage**	soup
		poulet	chicken
crêpes	pancakes	**ragoût**	stew
croûtons	cubes of fried bread	**réchauffé**	re-heated food
escalope	cutlet (often of veal)	**rôti**	roast
fraises	strawberries	**salade**	salad
framboises	raspberries	**saumon**	salmon
fricassé	re-heated food cooked in a white sauce	**sauté**	fried in butter
		veau	veal
fromage	cheese	**vol-au-vent**	pastry case with savoury filling
gâteau	a large rich cake		
glace	ice cream		
hors d'œuvres	an assortment of savoury salad foods, eaten at the start of a meal		

Entertaining friends

When you invite friends to your house for a meal, party or weekend visit, you are responsible for looking after them and making their visit enjoyable. You are the **host** or **hostess** and your friends are the **guests.**

The host and hostess should make their guests feel welcome. A cheery greeting at the door is always a good beginning.

If you have invited a few friends, introduce them to each other so that everyone knows everybody else and no one feels left out. Always see that guests have enough to eat and drink. When entertaining, it is safer to prepare too much food rather than too little. Guests should be encouraged to help themselves to the food and to mix freely. An informal and relaxed gathering is nearly always more successful than a formal and over-organized one. See that the room is well ventilated and that the room temperature is comfortable, and provide plenty of ashtrays.

Here is a list of suggested snack meals that are quick and easy to make when you are entertaining your friends:

1 Hot sausage rolls served with soup, potato crisps and onions.

2 Jacket potatoes served with cheese and tomato dips, and coffee.

3 Stuffed eggs, cold sausages on sticks, salted nuts served with soft drinks.

4 Scotch eggs and salad sandwiches served with cheese straws and glasses of milk.

5 Assorted pastes and fillings on cream cracker biscuits, onions and crisps. Serve with oatmeal scones and coffee.

If guests are staying overnight, the hostess should prepare the bedrooms beforehand. Here is a list of the preparations required:

1 Make the bed with clean sheets and pillowcases.

2 See that the room is ventilated but not too draughty; a portable heater should be handy if extra warmth is required.

3 Provide clean towels, one for each person.

4 Make a small flower arrangement for the bedroom; this will brighten up the room.

5 Leave some magazines or books in the room.

6 Check that there are sufficient coathangers and drawer space for your guests' clothes.

Can you think of other preparations which a hostess would be well advised to make?

Invitations

An invitation to a party is sometimes given over the telephone, or in conversation with your friends, but sometimes you may wish to write your invitation, particularly if your friends live some distance away. Written invitations can be *formal* or *informal.*

A formal invitation should be brief. It should tell the guest the date of the party, the time of the party, and where the party is being held.

It is courteous and proper to reply to a formal invitation in written form—even if you have already said that you will accept. The reply should be as brief as the invitation but the date, time and place, should be repeated to show that you are clear about the details. Wedding and 21st birthday invitations are usually sent by the parents and replies must always be addressed to the person sending the invitation.

Do you notice in the invitation the letters R.S.V.P.? Perhaps you will already know that they stand for 'Please reply' and come from the initials of the French words *Répondez s'il vous plaît.*

An informal invitation is usually in the form of a friendly letter or by word of mouth. Here is a written informal invitation and reply:

INVITATION

129 Rainbow close
Aspley

Miss Joan Hunt requests the pleasure of the company of Miss Anne Booth at a New Year's Eve Party, to be held on 31st December; at the Oak Tree Hotel, Bannington, commencing at 8p.m.

R.S.V.P.

INVITATION

129 Rainbow close
Aspley
20th December 1984

Dear Anne
I am having a NewYear's Eve party at the Oak Tree Hotel, Bannington and it would be nice to hear that you can come. The party starts at 8pm and I do look forward to seeing you then
Love
Joan

33 Bradbury lane
Colmarton

Miss Anne Booth thanks Miss Joan Hunt for her kind invitation to attend a New Year's Eve Party at the Oak Tree Hotel, Bannington, at 8 p.m., and has pleasure in accepting*
*(or .. regrets she is unable to accept because of a previous engagement).

REPLY

33 Bradbury lane
Colmarton
21st December 1984

Dear Joan
I have just received your letter and I am writing by return of post to let you know that I shall be glad to come to your party at the Oak Tree Hotel. Thank you for the invitation.
Love
Anne

REPLY   INFORMAL   FORMAL

Think and Do

1. Design an unusual menu card and write a suitable menu for a New Year's Day dinner.

2. Here is a place setting for lunch. The correct cutlery has been used but there are *five* mistakes in the place setting. Can you spot them?

3. List all the equipment that you will need to lay a table for four people. The meal is:

Salmon salad, bread and butter. Blackberry and apple pie, cream. Celery. Assorted cakes.

4. Draw a correct place setting for the following meals:

a. *breakfast* porridge; grilled bacon, tomatoes and mushrooms; toast and marmalade; coffee.

b. *dinner* oxtail soup; cheese and potato pie, grilled tomatoes, onion sauce; fresh fruit salad.

c. *high tea* hotpot, pickled cabbage, brussels sprouts; cheese and cream crackers; fresh fruit; Simnel cake.

d. *a wedding lunch* grapefruit; plaice in shrimp sauce; roast turkey, stuffing, sausage, Dûchesse potatoes, cauliflower, peas, gravy; sherry trifle; cheese and biscuits; coffee.

5. Design a suitable table decoration for:
a. a child's birthday party; *b.* a Christmas dinner; *c.* your parents' Silver Wedding tea; *d.* a buffet in summer.

6. Here are four meals. The dishes have been jumbled up. Re-arrange the dishes in each meal and write the meal out as it should appear on a menu.

a. Jam layer pudding, hotpot, gravy, brussels sprouts, custard, pickled cabbage.

b. Custard, toad-in-the-hole, pineapple sponge, gravy, mock turtle soup, turnips, cabbage, new potatoes.

c. Salad, stewed plums, bread and butter, cream, Scotch egg.

d. Mayonnaise, Cornish pasties, green salad, Queen of puddings, chipped potatoes.

7. An aunt has arrived for a surprise weekend visit. Suggest

a. a quick lunch that you could make from convenience foods in your larder, and

b. what preparations you would make in the spare bedroom.

8. Turn to the list of French cookery terms and try to work out for yourself the dishes in the meal shown in this menu.

9. Plan and then write neatly into your books, a formal wedding invitation. You may choose all the details yourself.

10. Look in magazines and try to find pictures of:

a. cutlery

b. a dinner service

c. a tablecloth

Stick them into your notebooks and underneath each one write the price of the object and why you like it.

11. You have invited a few friends for a record session. Suggest:

a. what food you would serve, and

b. what drinks you would provide.

12. If you were having the following snack meals at a self service café, what cutlery would you need to pick from the cutlery trays?

a. buttered scone, egg custard, cup of coffee.

b. hot dogs, chocolate biscuit, glass of orange.

c. fish and chips, bread and butter, cup of tea.

d. oxtail soup, cheese and cream crackers, glass of milk.

menu

Hors d'œuvres

Canard rôti
Pommes de terre
à la Duchesse
Petits pois
Salade d'oranges

Gâteau de pêches

Fromage

Part Two

All About Food

Chapter

5

Meat

In this section we shall learn more about the important foods that are used in planning meals. The first one we shall consider is meat.

A visit to your local butcher's shop will show you how many different kinds of meat there are. In this country we eat the meat from the cow, sheep and pig. Can you recognize the meat from each of these animals? Here is a simple chart to help you:

Animal		Name of meat	Appearance
COW	young	Veal	Pale pink in colour with white fat
	old	Beef	Bright red in colour with creamy fat
SHEEP	young	Lamb	Dull red in colour with hard white fat
	old	Mutton	Red with yellowish fat
PIG		Pork (Ham and Bacon)	Pinkish with soft, white fat

There is little flesh from any of these animals that is not eaten. A butcher sells brains, tongue, head, feet, liver, kidney, heart, tripe (which is the lining of the cow's stomach and intestines) and sweetbreads (which is the pancreas and throat glands of the sheep and calf), as well as the more usual cuts of meat. Can you think of any other parts of animals that you might find in a butcher's shop?

We must not forget to include in this section the birds such as chicken, turkey, goose and duck, which are all popular meats.

Food value

Meat is rich in animal protein. It is therefore an excellent body-building food. Can you remember the other four foods which are good sources of protein?

Try to imagine a joint of meat before it is cooked and you should be able to work out for yourself some of the other food nutrients which are present.

1 Meat contains **fat.**

2 Meat is moist and therefore it contains **water.**

3 Fresh meat oozes red blood and therefore it contains **iron,** which is the mineral that gives blood its red colour.

4 Meat is also rich in **vitamin B.**

Meat is therefore a very good buy as it is very nutritious and there are so many different kinds that meals need never be dull.

Cuts of meat

When deciding on what type of meat to buy for a meal, you must consider the length of time you will have available, because some types of meat require longer cooking than others. It is easiest to remember that cheap pieces of meat are usually tough and therefore require slow and careful cooking, whereas the dearer pieces of meat are more tender and require less preparation.

The slower methods of cooking suitable for cheaper cuts of meat are: **stewing, boiling.** The quicker methods of cooking suitable for dearer cuts of meat are: **grilling, frying.** Other methods are: **roasting, braising.** Roasting can be done in the oven or in a pot and the length of time needed depends on the size of the piece of meat. Braising is a mixture of stewing and roasting and can be used for either cheaper or dearer cuts of meat.

The sensible thing is to buy the right cut of meat for the

PROTEIN
VITAMIN B
IRON
WATER
FAT

dish you are preparing. It would be very extravagant to buy an expensive piece of meat for a stew, when a cheaper cut of meat would give just as good a result. Similarly it would be foolish to try and save money by buying a cheaper cut of meat, expecting it to be delicious when grilled. Can you imagine the result?

Here are diagrams of a cow, sheep and pig, and with each are listed some of the cuts of meat which are suitable for the different methods of cooking. Try to remember some from each group so that you will know which joint of meat to ask for when you next visit your butcher.

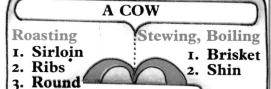

A COW

Roasting	Stewing, Boiling
1. Sirloin	1. Brisket
2. Ribs	2. Shin
3. Round	

Grilling, Frying
1. Fillet steak
2. Rump steak

(This meat is called BEEF)

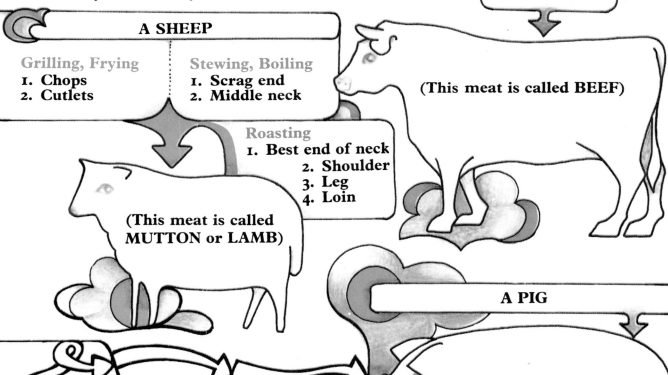

A SHEEP

Grilling, Frying	Stewing, Boiling
1. Chops	1. Scrag end
2. Cutlets	2. Middle neck

Roasting
1. Best end of neck
2. Shoulder
3. Leg
4. Loin

(This meat is called MUTTON or LAMB)

Stewing, Boiling	Roasting	Grilling, Frying
1. Flank	1. Loin	1. Chops
2. Hand	2. Leg	2. Steak

A PIG

(This meat is called PORK)

Structure of meat

When you next have a joint of meat for dinner, take a close look at it before it is carved. You will notice that there are long strips, or fibres, going in one direction. This is the **grain** of the meat. When carving the joint you should always cut across the grain. This will give you neater slices of meat.

Every kind of meat has these grains or fibres. The fibres are held together by a thin material called **connective tissue**, which before cooking is very tough. It is during cooking that the connective tissue is softened and this makes the meat easier to eat and digest.

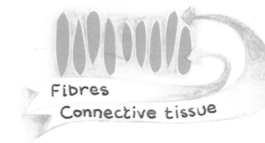

Fibres

Connective tissue

Why is meat cooked?

How many reasons can you suggest for cooking meat? There are three main ones. Cooking makes meat:

Danger! Germs at work

1 Food poisoning can be caused by eating meat that is not fresh. Never buy meat that smells or looks old. Be particular about your butcher. It is always best to buy from the butcher whose shops and assistants look clean and tidy.

2 Try to cook meat as soon as you buy it. If meat is to be left standing for a while, keep it in a cool, airy place, and always keep it lightly covered so that it does not attract flies.

3 Never partly cook a joint of meat and then re-heat it the following day. This can cause bad attacks of food poisoning. Germs will multiply in warm conditions and when meat is only partly cooked the inside of the joint is only warm and does not become hot enough to kill the germs. If a joint of meat is not needed until the next day, cook it through completely as soon as you have bought it and then store the meat in a cool place overnight.

4 It is especially important that joints of pork are completely cooked through because underdone pork can make you very ill.

easier to eat and digest

taste and look better

safer to eat

Accompaniments

During the Middle Ages much of England's wealth depended on the amount of wool it could sell abroad. In an attempt to stop the people from eating lamb, a royal command made it an offence to eat this meat without the herb known as mint. It was hoped that the bitter flavour of mint would make lamb unpopular so that more wool could be obtained and sold abroad. This law had the opposite effect. The flavour of the herb went so well with the taste of the meat that the tradition of eating the two together was established.

Different sauces improve the flavour of other meats so it has become usual to serve one with the other. Here is a list of the usual sauces and accompaniments for meat:

Meat	Accompaniment
Roast beef	Yorkshire pudding, horse-radish sauce or mustard
Roast lamb	mint sauce
Roast mutton	red currant jelly, onion sauce
Roast pork	apple sauce, sage and onion stuffing
Roast chicken	bread sauce, sausages, bacon rolls
Roast duck	sage and onion stuffing, orange sauce
Roast goose	sage and onion stuffing, apple sauce
Roast turkey	bread sauce, sausage or chestnut stuffing

It is not wrong to serve different accompaniments with meat, because it is really a matter of one's own likes and dislikes. There is no reason why mint sauce should not be served with roast beef. Choose a flavour of accompaniment that you like best.

Textured vegetable proteins (TVP)

Because meat is an expensive food, scientists have found a substitute by converting cheap vegetable proteins into products which look, taste and feel like meat. Textured vegetable proteins have vitamins and mineral salts added to improve their nutritional value. They can be used instead of meat or to make meat dishes go further.

We have now learned how to distinguish between different joints of meat and how to cook and serve them. Here are some suggested meat dishes for the main meals of the day.

Look them up in your recipe book and see how each of them is made.

Breakfast: Kidneys on toast; bacon with tomato; ham with egg; liver with mushrooms; sausages with apple rings.

Dinner or Lunch: Hotpot; mince collops; stuffed breast of lamb; roast heart; baked liver and onion; beefsteak pudding; curried beef; brown stew; beef olives; chicken casserole; mixed grill; moussaka; barbecued spare ribs.

High Tea or Supper: Meat and potato pie; tripe and onions; pickled brisket; Scotch eggs; veal and ham pie; Cornish pasties; pork pie; pâté; beefburgers; shepherd's pie; toad-in-the-hole; chicken supreme; lasagne.

Think and Do

1. Solve the following anagrams which are all cuts of meat:
ISBR; IORSILN; ARSEBT; RMUP; RSUELHDO; RETBKSI; FNALK; ILNO; NUDRO; TTECLU.

2. Are these sentences *true* or *false?*

a. Meat is rich in vitamin B.

b. There is no iron in meat.

c. Mutton comes from sheep.

d. Mint sauce is the correct accompaniment to serve with lamb.

e. Sirloin is a good joint of meat for roasting.

f. A joint of meat should be carved across the grain.

g. The meat from a young cow is called veal.

h. Cheap cuts of meat are used for frying.

i. Meat contains a large amount of starch.

j. The best cuts of meat should be used for stews.

3. Choose a meat from column B opposite to go with the correct animal in column A.

4. Visit your local butcher and find out the prices of the following meats:

a. a breast of lamb; *b.* 750 g joint of sirloin; *c.* 200 g sausages; *d.* 500 g stewing steak; *e.* 2 pork chops; *f.* 2 sheep's hearts; *g.* 200 g fillet steak; *h.* a loin of pork suitable for 4 people.

A	B
Pig	Lamb
Calf	Mutton
Sheep	Beef
Lamb	Veal
Cow	Pork

5. The following are suggested menus. Complete the first course with suitable accompaniments.

a. Roast chicken, ..., ..., ..., baked potatoes, peas, gravy. Apricot flan, cream.

b. Roast lamb, ..., jacket potatoes, cauliflower, gravy. Treacle sponge pudding, white sauce.

c. Roast pork, ..., ..., creamed potatoes, brussels sprouts, gravy. Baked Alaska with mandarin oranges.

d. Roast turkey, ..., ..., dûchesse potatoes, roast potatoes, celery hearts, beetroot in white sauce, gravy. Sherry trifle.

e. Roast mutton, ..., chipped potatoes, cabbage, gravy. Bread and butter pudding.

f. Roast beef, ..., ..., boiled potatoes, leeks, broad beans, gravy. Swiss apple pudding, custard.

6. Complete the crossword shown.

7. Suggest a suitable meat dish for the following:

a. a snack supper.

b. lunch for an invalid.

c. Sunday dinner for an old age pensioner.

d. a buffet party.

e. breakfast in a caravan.

f. a packed lunch.

g. a child's birthday party.

h. a wedding reception.

i. high tea for a policeman and his family.

j. lunch for a busy mother with a new baby.

8. Imagine you have a very limited housekeeping budget. Plan the week's meals for a household of four people using cheap cuts of meat. Work out a shopping list for all the meat you will require, giving amounts and approximate prices.

9. Describe briefly in your own words how you would:

a. make some mint sauce;

b. stuff and roll a breast of lamb;

c. skin some sausages for toad-in-the-hole;

d. carve a joint of beef.

10. Imagine you are planning a barbecue. Suggest a suitable menu. What entertainments would you plan to make the evening a success?

Clues across

1. The mineral salt present in meat
2. Meat from a sheep
3. The lining of a cow's stomach

Clues down

4. A joint of beef suitable for roasting
5. A method for cooking cheaper cuts of meat
6. A type of steak for grilling
7. Meat from a young cow

Chapter

6

Milk

The milkman on his daily round is a familiar figure to all of us. How many times have you stopped to wonder what life would be like without milk, the food which we take so much for granted?

Uses of milk

Milk has many uses in the home. Try to plan one meal without using milk and you will realize how difficult it is. Imagine breakfast time without any milk to put on your cereal and without any milk to put in your tea. Here are some of the main uses of milk. Can you think of any others?

1 Milk is the only food on which babies can grow.
2 Milk is used for making drinks (e.g. tea, coffee, drinking chocolate, milk shakes, etc.).
3 Milk can be drunk cold, i.e. without cooking.
4 Milk can be used in cookery for a variety of dishes (e.g. milk puddings, egg custards, white sauces, blancmanges).
5 Milk can be added to foods to make them creamier and improve their food value (e.g. creaming of potatoes, adding to cake mixtures).
6 Because milk is a liquid, it is very easy to digest and therefore it is a suitable food for invalids.

Food values

Milk is a very nutritious food. It is an animal protein and is therefore an important body-building food. Milk also contains some:

Fat for energy;
Sugar for energy;
Water for cleansing;
Vitamins A and *B* for protection. (There are small amounts of vitamins D and C present also.)

Milk is very rich in *calcium* which is the mineral salt necessary for healthy teeth and bones. There are traces of a few other mineral salts but very little iron.

Milk is not quite a 'perfect' food because it does not contain any *starch*. You can add to the food value of milk by serving it with a food that supplies this deficiency. For example, when making a milk pudding, milk is mixed with a starchy food (sago, rice, tapioca, semolina, etc.) and the food value is considerably improved.

Types of milk

Milk is produced by all female mammals to feed their young. In this country we drink the milk from cows but in other countries milk is also obtained from camels, goats and ewes. Can you think of any other animals which supply milk?

Milk has one main disadvantage as a food. It can easily become infected with germs. Care must be taken at the farm and at the bottling factory to keep milk pure and there are strict laws about how milk should be treated before it is sold to the public. Everything at the farm must be spotlessly clean. The cows are milked in hygienic surroundings and the milk is collected in sterilized, covered containers and taken to the bottling factory. Here it is tested to see that it is of good quality and then treated to make it safer to drink. One way of doing this is to heat the milk to a temperature of 71°C for 15 seconds

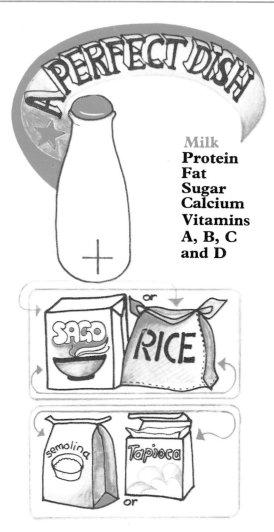

A PERFECT DISH

Milk
**Protein
Fat
Sugar
Calcium
Vitamins
A, B, C
and D**

PROTEIN CALCIUM
WATER SUGAR
MILK
FAT VITAMINS

and then to cool the milk rapidly to a temperature of 10°C. Milk which has been treated in this way does not contain any harmful germs and is safe to drink. This method of treating milk is called **pasteurization** after the French scientist, Louis Pasteur.

Homogenized milk is milk that has had its fat content broken down into tiny particles. This is done by warming the milk and forcing it through a fine hole. The milk is then pasteurized. Homogenized milk is easy to digest and is therefore suitable for very young children and for invalids.

Sterilized milk is milk that has been homogenized, bottled and sealed, and then heated to above boiling point (100°C) for 20 to 30 minutes to destroy **all** the germs present. This milk does not have the same fresh taste as pasteurized milk and the vitamin C is destroyed. Sterilized milk is sold in vacuum sealed bottles and will remain sterile for many days.

Channel Islands and South Devon milk is a rich, creamy milk which comes from the Jersey, Guernsey and South Devon breeds of cow. It contains a high proportion of fat.

Ultra heat treated milk will keep for several months, and is usually sold in date stamped aluminium foil containers. This milk has been homogenized and then heated to not less than 132°C for one second.

Milk may also be bottled at the farm without being heat treated. This type of milk is sold as untreated milk.

Here is a list of the different types of milk which you can buy from your milkman:

1 Pasteurized
2 Homogenized
3 Sterilized
4 Channel Islands or South Devon
5 Ultra heat treated
6 Untreated.

Milk can also be bought from your grocer in the form of:

1 evaporated milk
2 condensed milk
3 powdered milk.

These types of milk will keep indefinitely and are useful to have in the larder although they do not have the fresh goodness of natural milk.

Products from Milk

CHEESE
made from the curds of sour milk

BUTTER
made from the cream of milk

YOGHURT
made by treating milk with special organisms

CREAM

MILK

Products from milk

Milk can be used to make other foods. **Butter** is made from the cream of milk and **cheese** is made from the curds of sour milk.

Cream can be separated from the liquid part of milk and sold as *a* half cream, *b* single cream, *c* whipping cream, *d* double cream or sterilized cream.

Yoghurt is made by treating pasteurized, homogenized milk with special organisms. The milk is turned into a creamy, curd-like substance which has an acidic flavour.

Keeping milk fresh

1 Milk should be kept in a cool place especially in summer. If a refrigerator is not available the bottle of milk can be placed in a bucket or bowl of cold water and left in the shade. Milk should not be left on the doorstep for a long period of time because sunlight destroys the vitamins.

2 Milk will keep fresh in the sterile bottle in which it is delivered. If milk is poured into a clean jug it should be protected from dust and flies by a suitable covering.

3 Milk jugs should be rinsed in cold water before being washed in hot, soapy water. A regular scald with boiling water will keep the jugs sterile.

4 Empty milk bottles should be washed before being returned to the milkman.

5 In hot or thundery weather milk will quickly turn sour if it is not stored properly. Sour milk need not be wasted. It can be used for making scones if the amount of cream of tartar is halved (see chapter 16 on raising agents).

Ideas for using milk and its products

Why not experiment and try some of these unusual dishes. Make breakfast time different by having yoghurt and fresh fruit for a change and try the continental way of starting the day with coffee instead of tea. For dinner or lunch serve vegetables dressed in exciting white sauces (beetroot in onion sauce, cauliflower in cheese sauce, cabbage with mustard sauce, broccoli with egg sauce, diced cucumber with shrimp sauce, brussels sprouts with bread sauce, and turnips with horse-radish sauce.) Try green vegetables tossed in

cream instead of butter. Garden peas are particularly nice served this way.

For party dishes, fill pastry flan cases with savoury fillings in white sauce. They can be delicious. Try cooked ham with mushrooms, chicken with sliced hard-boiled egg and salmon with cucumber—all in white sauces. Bring milk shakes to life by adding crushed fresh fruit such as pineapple or banana and serve them sprinkled with chopped nuts. Bars of chocolate such as peppermint cream, melted in milk make unusual drinks to serve hot or cold.

The invalid can be tempted with small helpings of fish soufflé, chicken fricassée, plaice poached in milk, junkets, milk jellies, apple snow, baked custards, and egg nog. For these unusual dishes use the recipe books in your school library and see how each of them is made.

Think and Do

1. Collect pictures of milk dishes and stick these into your books under the heading MILK IS GOOD FOR YOU.

2. Prices of milk vary according to the type of milk and the season of the year. Find out the prices of the different types of milk just now.

3. Copy the following diagram into your books and supply the missing words:

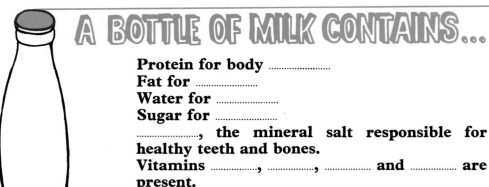

A BOTTLE OF MILK CONTAINS...

Protein for body ....

Fat for ....

Water for ....

Sugar for ....

................, the mineral salt responsible for healthy teeth and bones.

Vitamins ...., ..., ... and .... are present.

4. Copy this diagram into your books and write an appropriate sentence in each of the boxes.

FOOD VALUE

PRODUCTS

STORAGE

TYPES

5. Suggest a light lunch suitable for an invalid. Underline the dishes which use milk.

6. Copy the following paragraph into your books and supply the missing words:

'Milk is a .... food, and it is therefore body .... It is obtained from .... and .... Milk contains a mineral salt called .... which makes strong bones and teeth. Vitamins ...., ..., ... and .... are present. Milk contains a small amount of sugar but no .... and little iron.'

7. Complete the crossword puzzle in your books.

8. Write the following sentences into your book immediately underneath each other and use coloured crayon for the first letter of each sentence.

Points to remember for keeping milk fresh
May be easily contaminated.
In warm weather store in a cool place.
Loose milk bottle tops attract flies.
Keep milk in clean covered milk bottles or jugs.

9. Draw and colour a series of simple illustrations to show the stages through which milk passes before it reaches your doorstep. Here are some suggestions: a cow, a dairy shed, a milk lorry, a clean-looking factory worker, a labelled bottle of milk, the morning milkman, the doorstep of your house.

Clues across
1. This mineral salt is found in milk
2. Milk is a .... food
3. The liquid part of sour milk

Clues down
4. Butter is made from this
5. A milk pudding

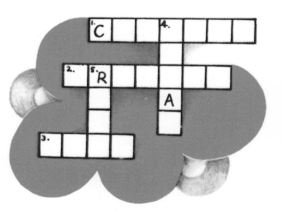

Chapter 7

Fish

Fish is not a favourite food with everybody because some people find it tasteless and prefer the stronger-flavoured foods such as meat and cheese. Fish has a delicate flavour but it can be a delightful food if it is cooked and served properly. In this chapter we are going to learn about the different kinds of fish and how to prepare attractive fish dishes for the members of the household.

Types of fish

There are three types of fish:

1 Oily fish; *2* White fish; *3* Shellfish.

1 Oily fish. As the name suggests this type of fish contains a large amount of oil or fat. The fat is in the flesh of the fish. Oily fish is difficult to digest because it is so fatty and for this reason it is not suitable for invalids.

Oily fish swim near the surface of the sea and are called **pelagic** fish. They get their food from the tiny plants in the water which are known as **plankton**. Oily fish are caught by nets which are dropped from fishing boats called **drifters**. Here are some names of well-known oily fish:

Herrings; salmon; pilchards, sardines; mackerel; eels.

How many of these would you be able to recognize in a fishmonger's?

2 White fish. The flesh of white fish does not contain any fat and so it is more easily digested. It is therefore a suitable food for invalids. There is a tiny amount of fat in the liver of white fish. White fish live at the bottom of the sea and are

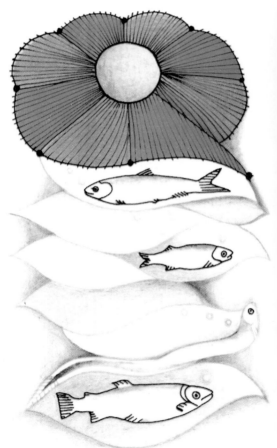

called **demersal** fish. They get their food from the sea bed. White fish are caught in nets which are dragged along the bottom of the sea by fishing boats called **trawlers.** Here are some well-known white fish:

Cod; plaice; haddock; turbot; halibut; whiting; sole.

Could you also recognize these?

3 Shellfish. Shellfish can be either partly or completely covered in a shell. The flesh of shellfish has tough fibres which are difficult to digest so this is not a suitable fish for invalids. The more common shellfish are:

Oysters; crab; lobster; prawn; shrimp; mussel; cockle.

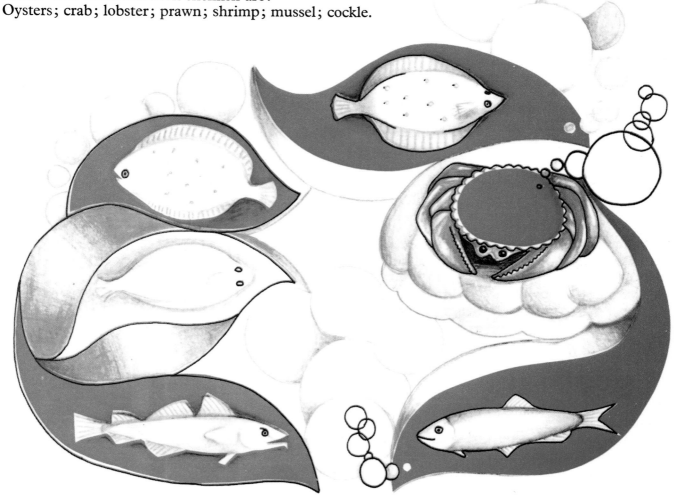

Food value

All fish is *protein.* Oily fish is very rich in fat and vitamins A and D. The mineral salts, phosphorus and iodine, are also present. White fish contains a large amount of water. There is a tiny amount of fat in the liver and small amounts of vitamins A and D. White fish also contains phosphorus and iodine. Shellfish is rich in protein but does not contain many vitamins or mineral salts. Tinned, oily fish, e.g. salmon, sardines and pilchards, where the bones of the fish have been softened by the canning process, contain good amounts of calcium.

Value for money

Oily fish is good value for money. It is a highly nutritious food and is equal in food value to meat. It is cheaper than white fish and has a stronger flavour.

White fish is not as economical because as well as being dearer than oily fish it is not as rich in fat and vitamins A and D. It has a delicate flavour which is often improved by serving with a sauce (e.g. parsley, cheese or anchovy sauce). Which do you think is the best buy for an old age pensioner— a herring or a fillet of plaice?

Buying fish

It is important that fish should be fresh when cooked. Old fish has a stale, unpleasant smell and must never be used. Always buy fish from a good, clean fishmonger's.

Fish can be bought as:

a whole fish; *b* fillets; *c* steaks or cutlets.

Small fish (e.g. herring and mackerel) are usually bought whole. The larger flat fish (e.g. plaice, sole and turbot) are sold as fillets, which are long thin pieces cut down the length of the fish and lifted off the bone.

There are four fillets to each plaice. If you want plaice for three people you would ask the fishmonger to give you three fillets of plaice.

Fish such as cod and hake which are long and round usually have steaks cut across the length of them. If you want hake for three people you would ask the fishmonger for three steaks of hake.

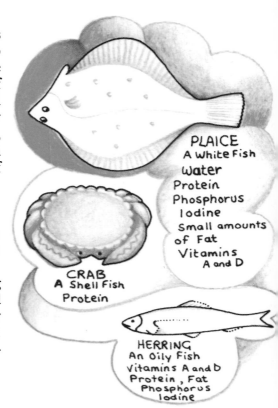

PLAICE
A White Fish
Water
Protein
Phosphorus
Iodine
Small amounts
of Fat
Vitamins
A and D

CRAB
A Shell Fish
Protein

HERRING
An Oily Fish
Vitamins A and D
Protein, Fat
Phosphorus
Iodine

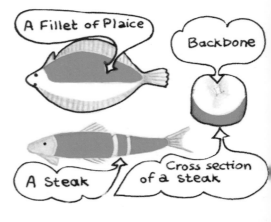

A Fillet of Plaice

Backbone

A Steak

Cross section of a steak

If you are not able to buy any fresh fish, then frozen fish is a good alternative. You can buy this from most grocers and supermarkets. It has all the goodness of fresh fish but is slightly more expensive to buy.

Tests for freshness

When buying fish always look for these points:

1 The fish should smell fresh.

2 Its eyes should be bright and prominent.

3 Any natural markings, such as the red dots on plaice, should be bright and clear.

4 The flesh of the fish should be firm to the touch.

5 The gills should be bright red in colour.

6 Crabs should be heavy in weight but dry when opened. (The fishmonger will remove the back of the crab if asked, to allow you to see that the crab is dry.) If there are any signs of water inside the crab it should be avoided.

Cooking fish

1 Fish should be cooked the same day that it is bought. If fish must be kept overnight use a refrigerator or leave the fish in a very cool place. Keep the fish covered.

2 Always wash fish under cold running water before cooking.

3 Fish is made up of flakes which are loosely bound together by a connective tissue. Care must be taken during cooking or the flakes of fish will fall apart. Boiling is not suitable for fish as the movement of the boiling water would break up the fish and spoil its appearance. Fish may be **baked, fried, steamed, poached** or **grilled.**

4 When cooking white fish it should be seasoned well. A little butter and a drop of lemon juice will also add flavour.

5 White fish should be served with a sauce. This adds flavour and texture to the dish. Here are some sauces to serve with fish:

Parsley sauce, cheese sauce, egg sauce, anchovy sauce, tomato sauce, shrimp sauce.

Can you suggest any others?

6 When fish dishes are garnished they can look very attractive. Some suitable garnishes are:

Water-lily tomatoes, sprigs of parsley, lemon slices, a few garden peas, gherkin rosettes, chopped chives, black grapes.

Ideas for fish dishes

Breakfast. **Why** not break the routine of bacon and eggs and, instead, have fish cakes for breakfast? They can be flavoured with salmon or tuna fish to make them more unusual. Try smoked haddock, kippers or risotto for a change.

Dinner or Lunch. Make a Russian fish pie for dinner and serve it with creamed potatoes, peas and egg sauce. Try baked stuffed plaice with chips, tomato baskets and parsley sauce. White fish can be made exciting by piping duchesse potatoes around an ovenproof dish and putting the fish in cheese sauce garnished with lemon, hard-boiled egg and gherkin.

High Tea and Supper. Try soused herrings with green salad; fish croquettes with beetroot in white sauce; dressed crab or fish and onion casserole.

Party dishes. For your next party experiment with salmon, tuna, prawns or crab meat in sauces. Try them in patties, puffs, choux pastries or flans, served with cooked rice or a green salad. Make sardine pyramids to serve hot or cold and flavour some stuffed eggs with anchovy essence. Seafood cocktails and paella can also be tried.

Think and Do

1. Here is a list of fish. Copy them into your books under the heading FISH IS RICH IN PROTEIN. Supply the missing vowels:
a. tr . . t; *b.* t . rb . t; *c.* s . l .; *d.* bl . . t . r; *e.* c . d; *f.* h . k .; *g.* pl . . c .; *h.* . . l; *i.* wh . t . ng; *j.* s . lm . n.

2. Complete the following menus, remembering to give a balanced meal which is varied in colour and texture:
a. Fish in batter, ..., ..., ...
    Apple crumble, ...
b. Fish fingers, ..., ..., ...,
    ...., custard.
c. Salmon flan, ..., ... Jelly, ...
d. Steamed plaice, ..., ..., ...
    Bakewell tart, ...

e. Grilled herrings, ..., ..., ...

........................., ...

f. Dressed crab, ..., ..., ...
Blackberry tart, ...

3. A seaside stall is selling the following shellfish. What are they?

a. SYESOTR; ***b.*** RABC; ***c.*** RSAWPN; ***d.*** TSLOSRBE; ***e.*** RHISMSP; ***f.*** SYFCAIRH; ***g.*** USMLSES; ***h.*** WSNIKEL; ***i.*** CLKOSEC; ***j.*** LSSACPLO.

4. Visit your local fishmonger's and find out the prices of the following:

a. a pair of kippers
b. a medium-sized crab
c. a fillet of plaice.
d. three steaks of haddock
e. 200 g cod
f. 2 smoked mackerel

5. You are preparing the following meal for a family of four. Write out your shopping list giving amounts and approximate prices. Russian fish pie, chipped potatoes, cauliflower, egg sauce. Stewed plums, custard.

6. List as many fish as you can think of beginning with the letters T and H.

7. Complete the following crossword:

Clues across
1. The food of pelagic fish
2. A group of fish
3. A cut to ask for when buying flat fish

Clues down
4. Smoked herrings
5. Found in the liver of white fish
6. A white fish
7. This mineral salt is present in all fish

8. Use your school library and find out as much as you can about one of the following subjects. Prepare an illustrated essay on the topic you have chosen.

a. deep sea fishing;
b. frozen fish—how it is done;
c. how to recognize different fish.

9. How would you serve the following dishes attractively:

a. fried fish cakes;
b. grilled herrings;
c. fried fillet of plaice;
d. crab;
e. poached, smoked haddock;
f. baked turbot;
g. fish pie;
h. tuna flan.

Chapter

Cheese

A visit to the cheese counter of a big supermarket or grocer's shop will show you how big a variety of cheeses there is to choose from. There are creamy-coloured, wheel-shaped ones, red-coloured tiny ones, blue veined cheeses and a variety of processed and packaged cheeses.

How cheese is made

The art of cheese-making has changed little through the years, and though most cheese is now made in big factories instead of in small farmhouses, the method is much the same.

Cheese is a dairy food. It is made from milk. In Great Britain cheese is made from cow's milk, but in other parts of the world milk from other animals, such as the ewe, goat and camel, is used.

Milk is soured by special organisms and then a substance called **rennet** is added. This causes the milk to separate into **curds** and **whey**. Can you remember the name of the nursery rhyme character who ate curds and whey?

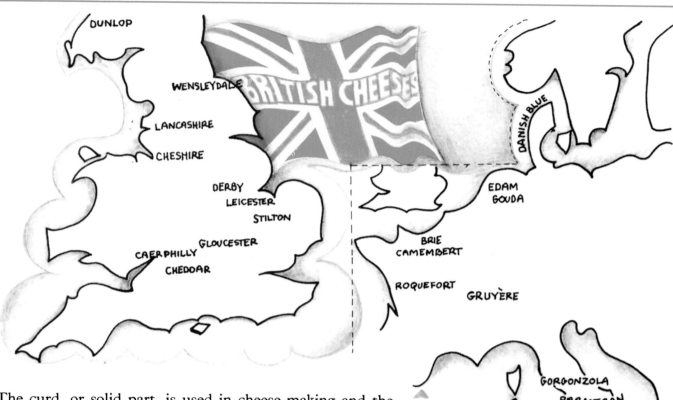

The curd, or solid part, is used in cheese-making and the whey, or liquid part, is drained off. Salt is added to the curd. This acts as a preservative as well as flavouring the cheese. The curd is then pressed into moulds and left to mature or ripen. If a very hard cheese is required the curd is pressed to squeeze out all the moisture, but if a soft cheese is needed some of the whey is left in the cheese. The amount of pressure, therefore, varies with the type of cheese to be produced. Can you name some hard and some soft cheeses?

As the cheese gets older its flavour develops. The flavour will depend upon the type of milk used, the climate and the age of the cheese. Some cheeses have colourings added to make them look more attractive and others have different 'trademarks'. The Swiss cheese called **gruyère** has holes punched in it. The Dutch cheese called **edam** is wrapped in a bright red skin. The Italian cheese called **gorgonzola** has a green mould growing in the cheese. Can you think of any other distinguishing marks in cheese?

You will have noticed from the maps on page 57 that many cheeses are named after the places where they were originally made. They may now be made in different areas also but they kept their original names as identifying marks so that people can recognize them.

Food value

Cheese is a very concentrated and nutritious food. Because cheese is made from milk its food value is similar to that of milk. A gallon of milk is used to make one pound of cheese. Cheese contains fat, water, the mineral salts calcium and iron, and vitamins A, B, and D.

Cheese consists of: $\frac{1}{3}$ protein; $\frac{1}{3}$ fat; $\frac{1}{3}$ water.
There is no **carbohydrate** or **vitamin C** in cheese.

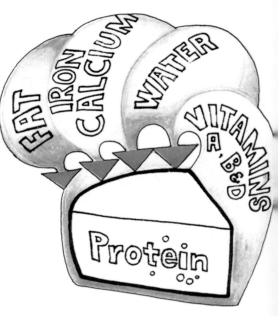

Digestibility

Cheese is a very solid food and because it contains a large amount of fat it is a difficult food to digest. There are many ways by which you can make cheese easier to digest.

1 If the cheese is cut up into small pieces, or grated, the fat is broken up and this makes the cheese more digestible.
2 If cheese dishes are seasoned well this helps also.
3 Cheese is made more digestible if it is served with a starchy food such as macaroni, potatoes or bread.

Cheese is not a suitable food to give an invalid because it is so difficult to digest. Which other body-building foods are more suitable for invalids?

Storage of cheese

Cheese can be wrapped in aluminium foil, 'cling-film' wrapping paper, greaseproof paper, waxed paper or polythene. It should be stored in a cool place. If a refrigerator is used the cheese should be left at room temperature for one hour before serving. Care should be taken to store cheese away from eggs to prevent the strong smell of the cheese penetrating the porous egg shells.

Any cheese which has become stale can be grated and either used in sauces or as a garnish for savoury dishes. If it is not required it can be stored in an airtight container and used when needed.

Buying cheese

It is important to be able to recognize the various cheeses so that you can choose the best type for the dish you intend to make. Some cheeses cook better than others and some cheeses grate more easily than others. **Hard cheeses,** e.g. Parmesan, Cheddar and Cheshire, grate easily and are therefore suitable for garnishing dishes and for adding to sauces and pies. **Soft cheeses,** e.g. Gloucester, Stilton and Caerphilly, do not grate easily. They are best when left in one piece and eaten with a salad or with savoury biscuits. Lancashire cheese has a very crumbly texture and is delicious when melted on toast and served as Welsh rarebit.

Processed and cream cheeses

There are many processed and cream cheeses available for sale in the shops. They are very useful as a base to spread on bread and savoury biscuits and can be decorated with an assortment of foods, e.g. tomatoes, radish, cucumber, gherkins and shrimps.

These cheeses have been made from ordinary cheese which has been melted. Various flavourings can be added to produce a different-tasting cheese, e.g. celery salt, curry, tomato and ham.

Processed cheeses can be stored in a larder indefinitely and are therefore useful as a standby food when catering for unexpected guests.

Cottage cheese

Cottage cheese is made from fat free milk. Lactic acid is used to form the curd, which is then heated, drained and washed. Salt and single cream are added.

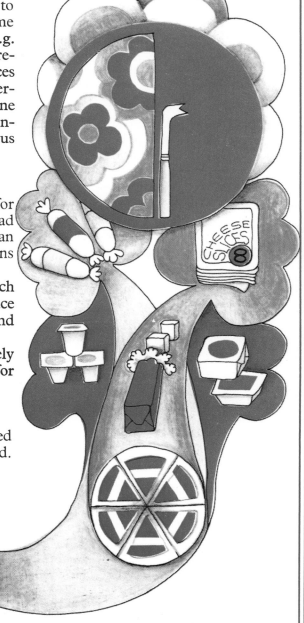

Ideas for cheese dishes

There are many exciting dishes which can be prepared using cheese. Try to find some new ways of serving cheese and be adventurous in tasting different cheeses. You will find what a delightful flavour some of them have. Here are some ideas for serving cheese throughout the day:

Breakfast. Cheese omelette; Welsh rarebit; cheese dreams.

Dinner and Lunch. Cheese and potato pie; cheese and vegetable hotpot; cheese pudding; Spaghetti Bolognaise with grated cheese; cheese soufflé; macaroni cheese; cauliflower in cheese sauce; eggs in cheese sauce.

High Tea and Supper. Cheese hamburgers; cheese and bacon pasties; stuffed cheese potatoes; cheese scones with sliced tomato or pineapple cubes; cheese and onion pie; cheese salad; cheese and tomato pizza; Quiche Lorraine; cheese Scotch eggs.

Party dishes. Cheese straws; cheese dip; cheese stuffed celery hearts; chicory with ham and cheese. Cheese also makes a good sandwich filling, e.g. stewed apple with grated cheese and chopped nuts; mayonnaise with grated cheese and pulped pineapple.

Think and Do

1. Copy this diagram into your scrapbooks and supply the missing words.

2. Suggest a suitable cheese dish for the following:
a. a picnic meal; *b.* a lacto-vegetarian's breakfast; *c.* a TV snack; *d.* dinner for a young family in winter; *e.* a buffet party savoury; *f.* a high tea in summer; *g.* an economical dish using hard cheese and left-over vegetables; *h.* a continental dish; *i.* a teenager's birthday party; *j.* a dish using cheese and pineapple.

3. Find out all you can about the following well-known cheeses and write a short paragraph about each:
a. Edam; *b.* Gorgonzola; *c.* Cheddar; *d.* Stilton.

4. Make a list of as many cheeses as you can think of beginning with the letters C and G.

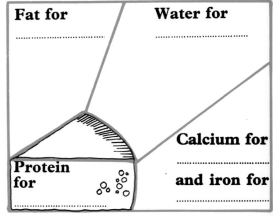

Fat for
....

Water for
....

Calcium for
....

and iron for
....

Protein for

Cheese also contains ....

5. Imagine you are a lacto-vegetarian, and plan a week's meals underlining all the cheese dishes in red. Underline the other sources of protein in green.

6. Solve the following anagrams. They are all well-known cheeses.

CEDHDRA; DAEM; ILOTTNS; DWAYLLENSEE; REYDB; MERNAAPS; TOECEUSLGR; ICRHHEES; ILURAPM; CIETEELSR.

7. How could you use up the following in attractive ways?

a. 200 g hard Cheddar cheese;

b. some cold cheese and potato pie;

c. some stale cheese scones;

d. 100 g grated Parmesan cheese.

8. You are preparing a cheese salad for 4 people. List the ingredients you would need to buy and work out the approximate cost of the salad.

9. Write a poem entitled 'The Cheese Counter'.

10. In order to have done the previous exercise you will have visited a cheese counter. Make a list of all the different types and kinds of cheeses that you saw. Find out the cost of each cheese and prepare your own price chart.

11. Solve the crossword puzzle.

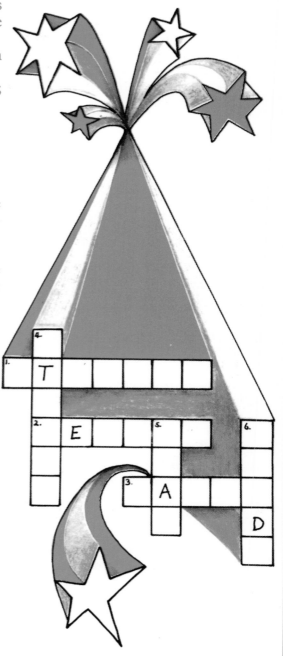

Clues across
1. A soft cheese
2. A substance found in the stomach of a cow
3. Cheese contains a large amount of this

Clues down
4. There is no .... in cheese
5. A Dutch cheese
6. The part of sour milk used in cheese-making

12. Look back at the map of British cheeses on page 57. Copy it into your book. Mark on it the names of towns you have visited (perhaps on holiday) in these cheese-making areas.

Chapter

9

Eggs

A well-stocked larder will usually contain plenty of eggs because these will provide quick and tasty meals. We are talking here about hens' eggs although, of course, there are other eggs, e.g. ducks', etc.

The hens

Hens are not all alike. They belong to different breeds or types. There are eight main breeds, the best-known being the Rhode Island Red, the Buff rocks and the White Leghorn. See if you can find out the names of the other breeds.

Hens can live in three different types of surroundings:
1 in batteries; *2* on the free range; *3* in a deep litter.

1 Battery hens live in row upon row of individual wire cages. The hens are provided with plenty of water and a balanced diet. The temperature of the battery is controlled and it is always well-ventilated. As the eggs are laid they fall into troughs from where they are collected.

2 Free-range hens are the hens you often see in fields close to farmhouses. They get their food from the grass in the field and have the benefits of fresh air, sunshine and exercise. Henhouses are provided and the hens return there to sleep and to lay their eggs. These eggs have a deeper coloured yolk than eggs produced in the other two types of surroundings but the food value is the same.

3 Deep litter hens live together in great numbers in special buildings. They are provided with a deep bed of a substance like peat as well as nesting boxes in which they can lay their eggs. They stay in these buildings until they can no longer lay eggs. The building is then emptied and thoroughly cleaned before the next batch of hens is brought in.

Can you suggest some advantages and disadvantages of each of these methods?

BATTERY HENS

DEEP LITTER HENS

FREE RANGE HENS

The eggs

Eggs have a fascinating life. Let us trace the journey one of them makes from the time it is laid to the time it reaches your breakfast table.

The new laid egg has a very rough shell. The shell must first be cleaned by the farmer, who carefully rubs it either by hand or in a special machine. Water cannot be used because the eggshell contains tiny holes and the water might pass through the holes and germs could infect the egg. The egg is then either sold to a local shop or sent to a packing station. These packing stations are regularly inspected and must be spotlessly clean and of a high standard. At the packing station the egg is carefully inspected for any faults. It is tested under a bright light which shows up any fault in the egg. This is called **candling.** If a fault is found in the egg it cannot be sold as perfect.

The perfect egg is put with other perfect eggs and grouped or graded according to size and quality. They are then put into boxes ready to be taken to the shops where you can buy the size you need.

Structure and food value

Eggs are very nutritious. They are good sources of animal *protein* and are therefore body-building. An egg can be divided into three parts:
1 the shell; *2* the white; *3* the yolk.

The shell of an egg consists of calcium carbonate but this is not edible. The white of an egg contains a large amount of *water.* The mineral salts *calcium, phosphorus* and *sulphur* are present. The yolk of an egg is rich in *fat, vitamins A, D* and *B,* and the mineral salt *iron.*

Eggs do not contain any *starch* or *sugar* so when eggs are served with a carbohydrate (e.g. bread, potatoes and sugar) their food value is improved.

Uses in cookery

Eggs have many uses in cookery.

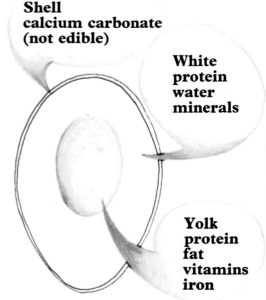

Shell
calcium carbonate
(not edible)

White
protein
water
minerals

Yolk
protein
fat
vitamins
iron

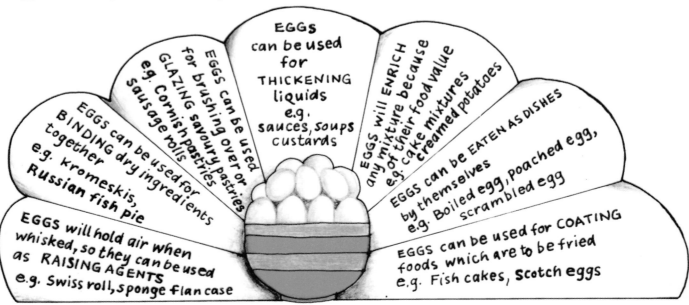

EGGS can be used for brushing over or GLAZING savoury pastries e.g. Cornish pastries, sausage rolls

EGGS can be used for BINDING dry ingredients together e.g. kromeskis, Russian fish pie

EGGS can be used for THICKENING liquids e.g. sauces, soups custards

EGGS will ENRICH any mixture because of their food value e.g. cake mixtures, creamed potatoes

EGGS can be EATEN AS DISHES by themselves e.g. Boiled egg, poached egg, scrambled egg

EGGS will hold air when whisked, so they can be used as RAISING AGENTS e.g. Swiss roll, sponge flan case

EGGS can be used for COATING foods which are to be fried e.g. Fish cakes, Scotch eggs

Tests for freshness

It is important to be able to recognize a fresh egg. Here are some simple tests which you can use to test the freshness of the eggs in your larder:

1 The shell of a fresh egg will feel rough.

2 A fresh egg will lie flat in a bowl of water but a stale egg will rise. This is because some of the water in the white of the egg will have evaporated through the holes in the shell, making the egg lighter in weight.

3 When a fresh egg is broken on to a plate, the yolk will be firm and the white thick and gluey. A stale egg will look runny, watery and will not hold its shape well.

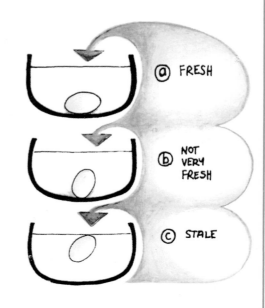

(a) FRESH

(b) NOT VERY FRESH

(c) STALE

Buying and storing eggs

1 Eggs should not be kept for a long time in the larder because they will quickly lose their freshness, go bad and begin to smell. It is best to buy eggs often in small quantities. The colour of shell varies according to the breed of hen which laid the egg and does not affect its food value. Brown-shelled and white-shelled eggs are equally nutritious.

2 Eggs in Britain are graded by size under EEC regulations and priced accordingly. Prices may change with the season. Size 4 is about the nearest to a standard egg (53–62 g).

Size 7	Size 6	Size 5	Size 4	Size 3	Size 2	Size 1
<45 g	45–50	50–55	55–60	60–65	65–70	>70 g

3 Eggs should not be stored near strongly-smelling food such as cheese or onions because the smell will pass through the holes in the eggshell and affect the taste of the egg.

4 Keep eggs in a cool place and store them with the blunt end uppermost. The yolk will then fall down into the shell to be surrounded by the white and kept fresh.

Cooking with eggs

Many people have eggs for breakfast but would not dream of having them for dinner, tea or supper. Here are some suggestions for eating eggs for each meal of the day. Some of these dishes may be new to you. Use the recipe books in your library to find out how each of them is made.

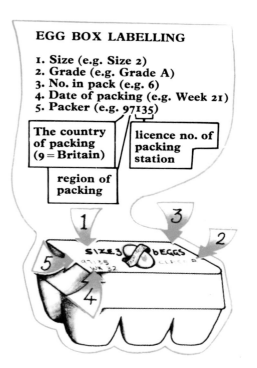

EGG BOX LABELLING

1. Size (e.g. Size 2)
2. Grade (e.g. Grade A)
3. No. in pack (e.g. 6)
4. Date of packing (e.g. Week 21)
5. Packer (e.g. 97135)

The country of packing (9 = Britain)

licence no. of packing station

region of packing

Breakfast. Poached egg on smoked haddock; cheese-flavoured scrambled egg; boiled egg with toast fingers; savoury omelette.

Dinner or Lunch. Egg and mushroom casserole; curried eggs; egg and tomato pie; Scotch eggs; egg kedgeree; eggs mimosa.

Tea or Supper. Quiche Lorraine; eggs au gratin; bacon and egg pie; poached egg in onion sauce; sandwiches soaked in beaten egg and fried until crisp.

Party dishes. Scrambled egg in tomato cases; stuffed eggs; egg croquettes; egg and chicken pasties. For sandwich fillings try: diced hard-boiled egg in mayonnaise; scrambled egg with chopped spring onions; scrambled egg with crushed pineapple and nuts.

Invalid dishes. Egg nog; coddled egg; poached egg on spinach; feathered egg; baked egg.

Having fun with eggs

Eggs are the subject of many interesting customs. The most well-known is the tradition of giving decorated eggs at Eastertime to relatives and friends. This custom started in China long before the Christian ceremony of Easter was first celebrated. Eggs were given by the Chinese each springtime to symbolize the re-awakening of life in the countryside. This Chinese custom gradually spread to other parts of the world until it was accepted by most countries. It was not until the middle of the 19th century that Easter eggs were made in chocolate and arranged in the colourful ribboned boxes that we know today. Why not try to decorate your own eggs next Easter? Use ordinary hard-boiled eggs and paint on them a simple colourful design.

The custom of having pace-egg races at Easter still persists in the North of England. In these races, coloured eggs are rolled down a hillside and there is always much rivalry between the competitors.

On Shrove Tuesday, pancake races are held in the streets of many towns and villages. The eating of pancakes marks the last day of feasting before the beginning of the fast for Lent. Any flour and eggs left in the pantry are used up in the making of the batter which is then fried into pancakes.

Think and Do

1. Collect pictures of egg dishes and stick them into your books under the heading EGGS ARE BODY-BUILDING.

2. Suggest a suitable egg dish for the following meals:

a. a supper to be eaten after an evening at the theatre;

b. a vegetarian's lunch;

c. a buffet supper;

d. breakfast for two campers;

e. a meal for a baby that has just been weaned;

f. a summer lunch to be cooked on a single gas-ring;

g. tea for a mother recovering from an operation;

h. a lunch that can be quickly prepared for an unexpected guest.

3. Design a poster to encourage people to buy and use more eggs.

4. Write a paragraph about each of the following:

a. free-range hens;

b. the egg-packing station;

c. the yolk of eggs.

5. Collect empty eggshells. Wash and dry them carefully and decorate them as attractively as you can. Prepare a class display under the heading 'Happiness is Egg-Shaped'.

6. Are these sentences *true* or *false?*

a. Brown eggs are more nutritious than white eggs.

b. A fresh egg will float in a bowl of water.

c. Eggs are rich in iron, the mineral salt that gives blood its red colouring.

d. The shell of an egg is porous.

e. Eggs do not contain any fat, so their food value is improved when served with fatty foods.

f. The average weight of a hen's egg is 25 g.

g. Candling is the name given to the method for testing eggs for faults.

h. Eggs are excellent sources of vegetable protein and are therefore body-building.

7. Plan a suitable menu for a New Year's Eve party. Include the following in your menu:

a. a savoury egg dish;

b. an unusual sandwich filling using eggs;

c. a cold sweet using eggs;

d. an egg drink.

8. Copy the following diagram into your books and complete the sentences in each of the boxes:

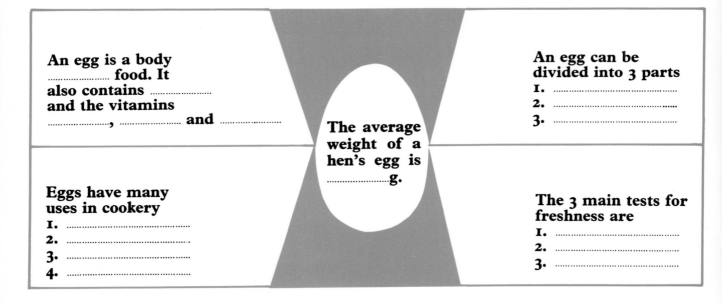

An egg is a body
.... **food. It**
also contains ....
and the vitamins
...................., ... **and** ....

The average weight of a hen's egg is .... **g.**

An egg can be divided into 3 parts
1. ....
2. ....
3. ....

Eggs have many uses in cookery
1. ....
2. ....
3. ....
4. ....

The 3 main tests for freshness are
1. ....
2. ....
3. ....

9. In your books draw and colour a suitable design for an Easter egg.

10. List as many different egg dishes as you can think of which would be suitable for breakfast.

Chapter 10

Fruits and vegetables

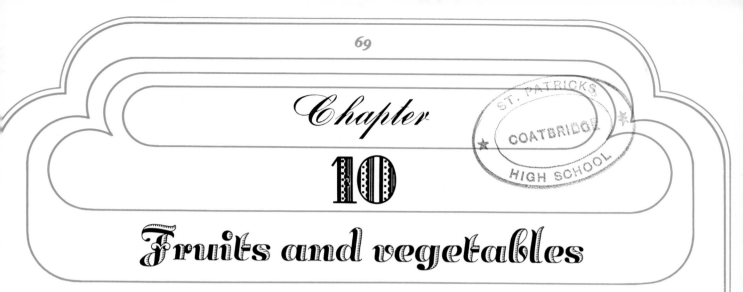

Fruits and vegetables often form a neglected and uninteresting part of our diet. Many people who willingly spend money on cakes and pastries do not seem to put as much importance on fresh fruit and vegetables. This is a great pity because fruits and vegetables are two of our best sources of vitamins and minerals salts, the nutrients which our bodies must have in order to remain healthy.

Always remember that fruits and vegetables are *valuable sources of vitamins and mineral salts.*
Why not give your family the protection of fruits and vegetables?

Can *you* think of a slogan to encourage people to buy more fresh fruits and vegetables?

FRUITS

Fruits can be divided into four groups:

1 Fresh fruit
2 Dried fruit
3 Tinned or bottled fruit
4 Frozen fruit

Food value

Fruits are good sources of:

Water is contained in all fruits except dried fruits. Because of the large amount of water present, fruits are good cleansing foods and have a very refreshing flavour.

Vitamin C is contained in most fresh fruits in small amounts. Very good sources of vitamin C are blackcurrants, roseships, strawberries and citrus fruits (oranges, lemons, grapefruit). Dried fruits contain little or no vitamin C. Tinned, bottled and frozen fruits do contain vitamin C.

Vitamin A is present in red- and orange-coloured fresh fruits, e.g. peaches, tomatoes, apricots, oranges. Vitamin A is also present in dried fruits, especially dried apricots and prunes.

Sugar and *dietary fibre* are present in all types of fruits in varying quantities.

Buying fresh fruits

1 Always buy fresh fruit from a good greengrocer. This should ensure that the fruits are reasonably fresh.
2 Try to buy fruits that are in season. Fruits are always cheaper when they are plentiful.
3 Fruits should look fresh and not be damaged or bruised.

Storing fruits

Fresh fruits do not keep well. If fruits are required for storing then buy tinned, bottled or dried fruits. If you wish to preserve some fruit yourself buy the fruit when it is cheap and just ripe. Over-ripe fruit is not suitable for home preserving. Fruit may be preserved by:

1 making jam or marmalade;
2 bottling;
3 drying;
4 freezing;
5 making fruit jellies;
6 making chutney.

Cooking fruits

Some people do not like the taste of fresh fruits but do like them when they have been cooked. When fruits are cooked some of the vitamin C is destroyed. To keep as much vitamin C as possible follow these directions:

1 Fruits which do not need skinning, e.g. gooseberries, damsons, blackcurrants, should be rinsed well before cooking.

2 Fruits which need to be skinned, e.g. apples, pears, peaches, should be peeled thinly and cooked immediately they have been prepared.

3 Fruits may be stewed in a saucepan with a tightly-fitting lid or in a casserole dish inside the oven.

4 Always add enough cold water to cover the bottom of the saucepan and enough sugar to sweeten (the amount of sugar to add will depend upon the fruit being used). Cook slowly. Stewed fruit should **not** be allowed to boil—it should simmer gently.

5 If you wish fruits to keep their shape during cooking, prepare the syrup first. Dissolve the sugar in the water and then cook the fruits slowly in the syrup.

6 When stewing dried fruits, **more** water is required than when stewing fresh fruits, but **less** sugar. The length of cooking time will be longer than for cooking fresh fruits.

Ideas for serving fruit
1 Raw fruits make a delicious finish to any meal and are particularly refreshing at breakfast-time.
2 Stewed fruits may be used in pies, flans, tartlet cases and be decorated with fresh cream or custard.
3 Fresh fruits can add colour and texture to a vegetable salad. A lettuce, orange and nut salad goes well with most foods. Which other fruits could you add to a vegetable salad?

Fruit salads
Fresh fruits can be cut into small pieces and served in a syrup as a fruit salad. This is a very refreshing sweet and is delicious when chilled and served with fresh cream or ice-cream. Try to add colour to your fruit salad. Black grapes, cherries and strawberries can add bright splashes of colour when mixed with the yellow and white of bananas, oranges, apples and pears. Tinned fruits can also be added to a fresh fruit salad to give more variety both in colour and in texture.

Fruit dishes
Why not try some of the more unusual ones?
Gooseberry fool, apple snow, banana flan, bilberry tart, blackberry summer pudding, prune mould, fruit in jelly, apple fritters, melon with ginger, peach amber, apple charlotte, orange trifle, lemon soufflé, strawberry gâteau, blackcurrant mousse.

VEGETABLES

Vegetables can be divided into groups according to their type:
1 Root vegetables;
2 Pod or pulse vegetables;
3 Green vegetables.
Root vegetables grow beneath the ground, e.g. potatoes, parsnips, carrots, swedes, beetroot and radishes.
Pod or pulse vegetables as their names suggest, grow in pods, e.g. peas, beans, lentils.
Green vegetables are the vegetables whose green leaves are eaten, e.g. cabbages, lettuces, brussels sprouts, chicory, cress and spinach.

Food value

The food value of each vegetable varies but it is easy to remember that most vegetables contain:

Vitamins; mineral salts; water; dietary fibre.

The following nutrients are present in the different groups of vegetables:

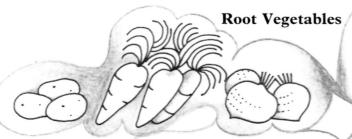

Root Vegetables

Mainly Starch
Some Sugar (beetroot, carrots)
Vitamin A (carrots)
a little Vitamin C
(potatoes, especially new potatoes)

Pod or Pulse Vegetables

Protein
A little Starch
Some Iron (peas, beans)
Some Vitamin B (peas, beans)
Fat
Oil

Buying vegetables

1 Always buy vegetables from a good greengrocer. Try to find one that has plenty of customers because this means that there will be a regular delivery of fresh vegetables to the shop.
2 Root vegetables should not look withered or spongy in appearance. Their skins should be bright and firm.
3 Green vegetables should look crisp and fresh.
4 Pod vegetables should look and feel full. These should be firm and dry to the touch.
5 Cauliflowers should have a firm, white head and not be yellow in colour.
6 When buying potatoes see that they are free from soil as this will only be weighed with the potatoes and give extra weight. Note that red-skinned potatoes (e.g. King Edwards) boil well and white potatoes cook well in fat.

Storing of vegetables

1 Do not try to keep vegetables for a long time before cooking them.

Green Vegetables

Good source of Vitamin C
Vitamin B
Calcium
Some Iron

2 Green and podded vegetables keep best in the dark. Either wrap them in newspaper or place them in a saucepan with a tightly-fitting lid. If just being kept for a day or two lettuce can be washed and either placed in the crisper of a refrigerator, or put in a lidded saucepan that has a little cold water in the bottom.

3 Root vegetables keep best if they are placed in a vegetable rack so that air can circulate round them.

Preparing vegetables for cooking

1 Green vegetables should be soaked for a few minutes in a cold water and salt solution. This will help to remove any insects or grubs. Rinse well before cooking.

2 Root vegetables should be peeled thinly and then washed well.

3 When slicing or chopping vegetables, use a sharp-bladed vegetable knife and cut the food into even-sized pieces.

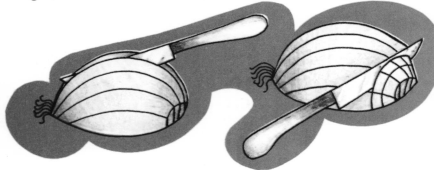

Cooking vegetables

Vegetables are cooked in order to soften them and make them more digestible. During cooking the mineral salts present in the vegetables are lost into the cooking water and the vitamin C is often destroyed.

To prevent the loss of the mineral salts:

Either cook the vegetables in a **casserole** or **stew,** so that the liquid is served as part of the dish,

Or use the cooking liquid to make a **gravy** or **soup.**

To prevent the loss of vitamin C:

1 Place the vegetables in **boiling** water instead of in cold water.

How to store Vegetables

CABBAGE IN NEWSPAPER ....

2 Cook in a **small** amount of salted water.

3 Cook **quickly** with the lid on the pan.

4 Do **not** add bicarbonate of soda to the cooking water. (This used to be added when cooking green vegetables to improve their colour but it destroys the vitamin C present.)

5 When cooked, drain and serve the vegetables **immediately;** do not try to keep them hot.

NOTE. Vegetables may also be **steamed, roasted, baked,** or **cooked in a pressure cooker.**

Ideas for serving vegetables

1 When serving vegetables add a knob of butter and sprinkle well with chopped parsley. This will add flavour, food value and make the dish look more attractive.

2 Serve vegetables coated in a well-flavoured sauce.

3 Heat a can of condensed soup and pour this over the vegetables just before serving. Celery, mushroom and tomato soups make delicious sauces to serve with vegetables.

A word about potatoes

Instead of serving boiled potatoes, or chips, try one of these different ways of cooking potatoes:

1 Bake potatoes in their jackets.

2 Boil potatoes in their jackets. Then skin and toss the potatoes in chopped parsley and butter.

3 Cream potatoes with butter and egg. Pipe the mixture on to a tray in fancy shapes and brown in a moderate oven.

4 Cream potatoes with egg and milk. Shape the mixture into balls and coat in egg and breadcrumbs. Fry in deep fat until golden brown.

Duchesse potatoes

WHAT TO USE WHEN COOKING VEGETABLES

SALT

WATER

A TIGHTLY FITTING LID

COOK OVER A HIGH HEAT

5 Boil potatoes for 10 minutes. Slice and place them in an ovenproof dish. Cover with a savoury egg custard and bake until set.

6 Cream potatoes and mix with finely-grated cheese and onion.

Vegetable salads

Salads can be made from uncooked vegetables, cooked vegetables or a mixture of both.

The usual green or summer salad, consisting of lettuce, tomato and cucumber can be served with most dishes. It can accompany cold meats, or just as easily be served with a hot meal.

Vegetables, such as cabbage, cauliflower and carrots, are delicious when served raw in a salad. They may be diced, shredded or sliced. They may be tossed in salad cream, served with oil or vinegar, or just served raw.

Left-overs of cooked vegetables can often be added to salads to disguise the fact that they are left-overs.

Do not forget to add nuts, raisins or dates occasionally to your salad. They will add interest and food value.

Using frozen, tinned and dried vegetables

1 Frozen vegetables should be cooked in boiling, salted water. A better flavour is obtained if the vegetables are **not** allowed to thaw before they are cooked. Do not overcook frozen vegetables. Serve them immediately they are ready.

2 Tinned vegetables should be strained before being heated through thoroughly in salted water.

3 When using dried vegetables read the directions on the packet carefully. You must cook the vegetables for the length of time suggested so that they absorb enough moisture to make them soft and digestible.

Vegetable dishes for you to try

Here is a list of dishes using vegetables. How could each of these dishes be turned into a complete meal?

Vegetable hotpot; vegetable pasties; vegetable flan; cooked vegetables in an egg custard; stuffed marrows (cucumbers or cabbages); curried vegetables; vegetable broth with dumplings.

Think and Do

1. The following is a vegetable salad. Of what does it consist ?
a. UMEUCBRC; *b.* SECRS; *c.* OINNO; *d.* CTELTUE; *e.* RATCOR;
f. EOEOTTRB.

2. List as many vegetables as you can think of which begin with the letters C and P.

3. You are anxious to give your family plenty of fresh fruit but they dislike its flavour. How could you prepare each of the following so that they would enjoy the dish ?
a. bananas; *b.* oranges; *c.* lemons; *d.* strawberries; *e.* black-currants; *f.* gooseberries; *g.* damsons; *h.* grapefruit.

4. Imagine you are preparing a fresh fruit salad for a family of four. List the ingredients and amounts that you will need. What will be the final cost of your fruit salad ?

5. Visit your local greengrocer and find out the current prices of the following:
a. a large turnip; *b.* 500 g brussels sprouts; *c.* 1 kg cooking onions; *d.* a bunch of spring onions; *e.* one head of celery; *f.* 2 kg potatoes; *g.* 500 g carrots; *h.* a marrow.

6. How could you sensibly use up the following left-overs ? Suggest a different dish for each item.
a. mashed potatoes; *b.* cooked peas; *c.* half a tin of pears; *d.* cooked cabbage; *e.* stewed apple; *f.* cooked beetroot.

7. List as many different ways of cooking potatoes as you can think of.

8. Either visit your local greengrocer or use the reference books in your library to find out the months of the year when the following foods are in season and at their best:
a. celery; *b.* brussels sprouts; *c.* peaches; *d.* radish; *e.* leeks; *f.* strawberries; *g.* sweetcorn; *h.* raspberries; *i.* spring onions; *j.* Savoy cabbage; *k.* gooseberries; *l.* Cox's orange pippins.

9. Complete the crossword in your notebooks.

10. Suggest ways of cooking and serving the following vege-tables attractively:
a. cauliflower; *b.* cabbage; *c.* runner beans; *d.* leeks; *e.* parsnips; *f.* beetroot.

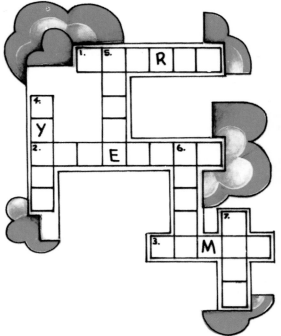

Clues across
1. A root vegetable
2. Berries which are rich in vitamin C
3. Citrus fruit

Clues down
4. Fruit may be stewed in this to retain its shape
5. A fruit which turns brown when peeled
6. Type of vegetable
7. Must not be added when cooking green vegetables

Chapter

11

Fats and oils

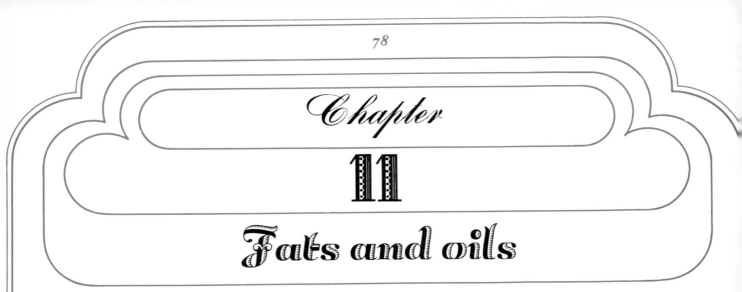

Fats and oils are used in cookery for:
1 Frying food.
2 Greasing cake tins.
3 Adding richness to cakes, biscuits and pastries.
4 Serving with bread, savoury biscuits and some pastries.
5 Serving with salads.

The difference between fats and oils
Fats are **solid** at a normal temperature, whilst oils are **liquid.**

Food value of fats and oils
Fats and oils are **energy-giving** foods. They supply our bodies with energy for work and heat. The amount of fat that each person requires in a diet will vary. People living in cold climates need more fat than people living in the hot regions of the world. A suitable breakfast for a cold winter's day in Britain might be: fried bacon, egg and tomato, toast and marmalade; but this type of 'fatty' breakfast would not be suitable for people living in hot countries such as in parts of Africa and Central America. People in hot climates need far less energy-giving food than we do. Most fats and oils also contain vitamins A and D.

FATS

Fats can be divided into two groups:
1 *animal* fats; 2 *vegetable* fats.
  Animal fats are those fats which we obtain from animals (e.g.

butter, lard, dripping, and suet). Vegetable fats are those fats which are manufactured from vegetable oils (e.g. some margarines and white cooking fats).

Butter

Butter is made from the pasteurized cream of milk. It is churned well in a large machine and this separates the fat from most of the water in the cream. The fat is then pressed to remove more of the remaining water. Salt is often added to butter at this stage because it adds flavour and helps the butter to store well. Colouring may also be added to give the butter a rich, yellow appearance. The pressed and salted butter is then cut, weighed and wrapped in blocks ready to be sold in the shops.

Butter is often preferred to margarine because:

1 It has a distinct flavour.
2 Cakes made with butter keep moist and store better than cakes made with margarine.

Butter is more expensive to buy than margarine. Two countries that are well known for the butter they produce are Denmark and New Zealand. Do you know the current prices for 250 g Danish butter and 250 g New Zealand butter?

Lard

Lard is a white fat and comes from the pig. It is the fat from the inside of the animal. The fat is melted down and cleaned thoroughly before it is cooled and prepared for the shops. Lard can be bought in packets or loose.

Lard is a **pure fat.** It does not contain any water therefore it is a very rich fat. It is good to use when making pastry

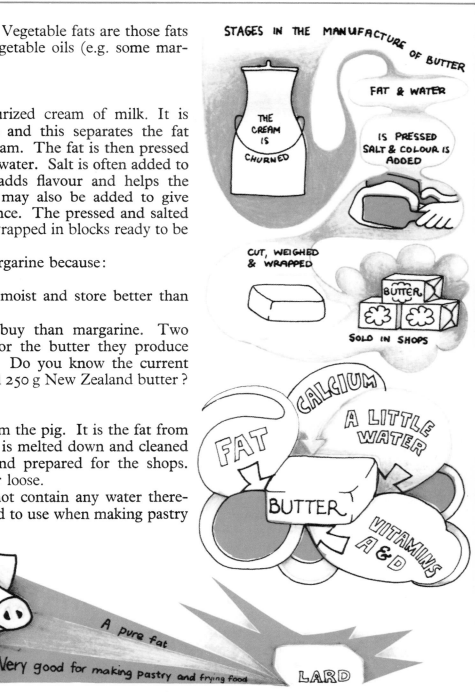

STAGES IN THE MANUFACTURE OF BUTTER

THE CREAM IS CHURNED

FAT & WATER

IS PRESSED SALT & COLOUR IS ADDED

CUT, WEIGHED & WRAPPED

BUTTER

SOLD IN SHOPS

FAT

CALCIUM

A LITTLE WATER

BUTTER

VITAMINS A & D

A pure fat

Very good for making pastry and frying food

LARD

because its richness gives a short and crumbly texture to the pastry. It is also a good fat in which to fry foods. Lard has a strong flavour and for this reason it is not suitable to use when making cakes.

Dripping
Dripping is the melted fat from other animals apart from the pig. It has been strained to remove any skin and is a **pure fat.** It has a strong 'meaty' flavour which makes it unsuitable for using in cakes and pastries. It is useful, though, when cooking meats and vegetables.

Suet
Suet is obtained from sheep and cows. It is the fat which surrounds the heart, liver and kidneys. Suet from sheep (mutton suet) is very hard and it has a strong flavour. Suet from cows (beef suet) is a softer fat and has a milder flavour.

Suet is a very solid fat and it is hard to digest. It should always be cut into small pieces, or chopped finely, before being used in pastries, mincemeat, etc. Suet can be bought already cut up. This is called **shredded suet.** Shredded suet is much easier and quicker to use than raw butcher's suet, but it is much dearer in price.

Margarine
Margarine is a man-made fat. It was first made in France by a man called Mège-Mouriès. In 1870 France was at war with Prussia (part of the country we call Germany). Food was scarce in France and many food substitutes had to be used. Mège-Mouriès carried out many experiments to try to make a substitute for butter. After many attempts he produced a margarine which he had made by squeezing animal fats and mixing them with milk. This early form of margarine was whitish in colour, like a pearl, and so it became known as **margarine** (after the Greek word meaning 'a pearl' which was **margaron**). Today margarine is made from a mixture of animal fat, fish oil and vegetable oil. Some soft margarines are made purely from polyunsaturated vegetable oils. These are low in cholesterol and help to reduce the risk of heart disease.

Mutton Suet (a hard fat with a strong flavour)

Beef Suet (a softer fat with a milder flavour)

HAS ALREADY BEEN CHOPPED FINELY

IS EASY TO USE

Shredded Suet

IS DEARER THAN RAW SUET

Margarine, by law, must have vitamins A and D added before it can be sold to the public. This improves its food value considerably. Some margarines also contain small amounts of butter fat to improve their flavour. Colouring may also be added to give a better appearance.

Margarine is cheaper to buy than butter. It is suitable for making cakes and pastries, and is often very easy to cream.

White cooking fats

These cooking fats are also made from vegetable oils. They do not have any vitamins or colouring added. White cooking fats cream easily and quickly mix into flour when making pastry. Pastry, made with these fats, is very rich and short.

OILS

Oils are sold in their liquid form. They are rather expensive to buy but have some definite *advantages* over solid fats.

1 Oil which is used for frying can be used over and over again, and does not deteriorate or go bad with keeping, as happens with solid fats such as lard.

2 Foods fried in oil are more digestible. Corn, sunflower and safflower oils are rich in polyunsaturated fats.

3 Oil can be heated to a higher temperature than fats before it starts to smoke.

4 Oil is sold in sealed bottles which can be used for storing the fat after it has been used for frying.

The oil obtained from olives (olive oil) is used for making salad cream and salad oils. (It is also used in soap-making).

It is interesting to know that vegetable oils may also be used for making plastics, linoleum, some paints and inks, food products for animals, and cosmetics.

Storing oils and fats

After using fats and oils, they should be strained through a piece of muslin or a sieve. This will remove any crumbs of food and the fat will keep fresher. Always keep fats and oils in a cool place.

Think and Do

1. Collect the wrapping papers from as many vegetable fats as you can find. Wipe them clean. Stick them neatly into your books, and underneath each one write:
a. the price of the fat, and *b.* the colour of the fat, e.g. dark, yellow, pale yellow, creamy white.

2. Find out all you can about how margarine was first made, and write a short description in your books explaining the history of margarine from its discovery to your collection of present-day wrappers.

3. Visit your local butcher and ask if you may see some beef suet and some mutton suet. Write down as many differences between the two suets as you can see.

4. Which fats or oils would you use for each of these dishes?
a. dumplings; *b.* Christmas cake; *c.* scones; *d.* flaky pastry; *e.* the frying of Scotch eggs; *f.* salad cream; *g.* roast beef; *h.* jam layer pudding.

5. Which is the odd one out in the following groups? Why?
a. Butter, lard, margarine, dripping.
b. Soya bean, lentil, coconut, groundnut.
c. Butter, cheese, yoghurt, suet.
d. A plastic rattle, a pencil, a piece of linoleum, a block of soap.

6. Are the following sentences *true* or *false?*
a. Fats and oils are body-cleansing foods.
b. Fats can be divided into two groups—vegetable and mineral.
c. Butter, lard and dripping are vegetable fats.
d. Butter is made from the cream of milk.
e. Vitamins B and C are added to margarine during manufacture.
f. Lard comes from sheep.
g. Beef suet is softer and has a milder flavour than mutton suet.
h. Margarine is a man-made fibre.
i. Olive oil is used for making salad cream.
j. Polyunsaturated fat reduces the risk of heart disease.

7. Visit your local grocer and find out the prices of the following:
a. 250 g shredded suet; *b.* 500 ml of olive oil; *c.* 500 g New Zealand butter; *d.* a small bottle of frying oil; *e.* 250 g of a margarine that contains 10% butter.

8. Copy the following sentences into your books using the correct word which you will choose from those words in the brackets:
a. Suet is the fat that surrounds the (eyes, internal organs, leg joints) of sheep and cows.
b. (Monte Cristo, Maigret, Mège-Mouriès) was the first person to make margarine.
c. Butter is made from (cream, curds, cod liver oil).
d. Lard is a white fat which comes from the (cow, lamb, pig).
e. Margarine was first made from milk and (vegetable oils, suet, animal fats).

9. Imagine that you have been asked to plan a New Zealand Butter Fortnight. Suggest some ideas you could try to encourage people to buy New Zealand butter.

10. Copy the chart into your note-books and write a suitable sentence in each of the boxes.

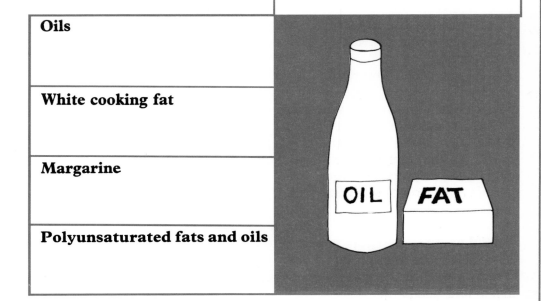

| **Butter** |
| **Lard** |
| **Dripping** |
| **Suet** |

| **Oils** |
| **White cooking fat** |
| **Margarine** |
| **Polyunsaturated fats and oils** |

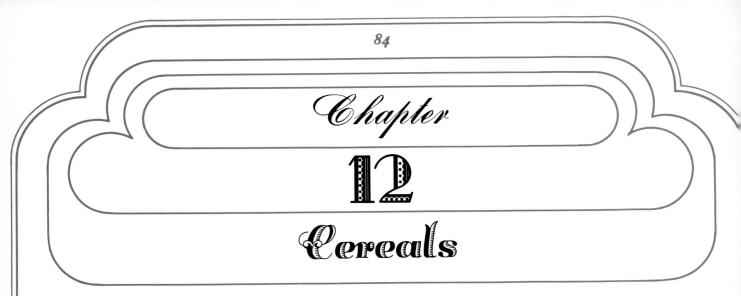

Chapter 12

Cereals

Ceres was the Roman goddess of the harvest. It is from her name that we get the word *cereal*. Cereals are the seeds of certain grass plants which are grown in many parts of the world for the food they give.

There are six main cereals: wheat, maize, oats, barley, rye, and rice.

These cereals can only be grown in countries where there is a suitable climate.

Wheat is a cereal that grows best in extremes of temperature. It likes a hot dry summer and a cold winter. The main wheat-growing countries of the world are U.S.S.R., U.S.A., India, China and Canada as well as parts of Britain, Europe and Asia.

Maize is a cereal that prefers hot but moist climates such as in Brazil, Mexico, parts of South Africa and the U.S.A. Maize is also known as sweet corn.

Oats can grow in many different climates but the main oat-growing countries are in the northern hemisphere (i.e. lands north of the equator) such as U.S.A., Canada, and the countries of Europe and Asia.

Barley is grown in Britain and in other countries with similar climates.

Rye is grown in many of the North European countries, e.g. Poland and it is particularly suited to the Russian climate.

Rice is a cereal that prefers a very hot but moist climate and it grows well in the countries of Asia, such as China, India, Japan and Thailand.

Have a look at a map of the world and find the countries where each of these cereals is grown.

Structure and food value

A grain of cereal consists of three parts:

1 the outer covering or **husk;**

2 the inside or **starch kernel;**

3 the **germ.**

Cereals are not very rich in nutrients. They contain:

carbohydrate (in the kernel)

a little **vitamin B** (in the husk and the germ)

small amounts of **vegetable protein** (in the germ)

small amounts of **fat** (in the germ)

dietary fibre

Their food value is improved considerably when cereals are served with a protein food such as milk, eggs or cheese, e.g. milk puddings, bread and butter pudding, macaroni cheese. When cereals form the main part of a diet as is still the case in many countries of South East Asia, the diet lacks **animal protein, vitamins** and **mineral salts.**

Because cereals are rich in carbohydrates, they are excellent **energy-giving foods.** They keep well and are cheap to buy. For these reasons cereals are often important foods in a country's diet and are known as 'staple' foods. The following are examples:

Wheat is the staple food of European countries, Canada and U.S.A.

Rye is the staple food of Russia.

Rice is the staple food of China and India.

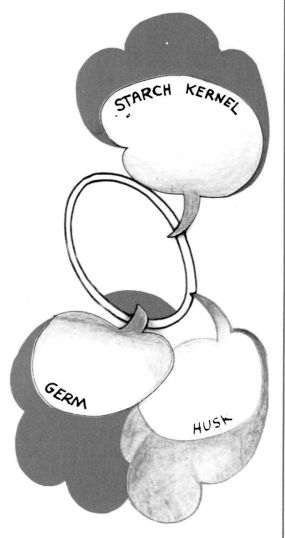

Products from cereals

1 Breakfast cereals. There are many different kinds of breakfast cereals for you to choose from. They can be made from wheat, maize, oats or rice. They have the nutrients which are present in raw cereals and the benefit of extra vitamins and mineral salts which are added during manufacture. If the breakfast cereals are served with milk and sugar, extra food value is added and the result is a satisfying and nutritious food.

2 Flour is made from wheat. The wheat grain is ground,

sieved and washed. The outer husk of the grain and the germ are removed, so that a fine, white flour can be made. Some flours have the germ and parts of the husk left in and these are called 'wholemeal' flours. Germ-enriched flour is white flour with added germ. Flour is made into bread, cakes, biscuits and pastries. Do you prefer bread made from white flour or wholemeal flour? Why?

3 Spaghetti and macaroni. These are made in Mediterranean countries such as Spain and Italy. They are made from a flour and water paste which is shaped in long, thin tubes and then baked. Spaghetti and macaroni usually accompany savoury dishes.

4 Oatmeal is prepared from oats. The grain is ground between heated rollers and sold as either rough, medium or fine oatmeal. It is used for making parkins, porridge and oatcakes.

5 Pearl barley is made from barley. The grain is polished to remove the outer husk. Pearl barley can be used for thickening and flavouring soups, stews and casseroles.

6 Cornflour is made from the inner part of the maize grain. It can be used for thickening gravies, sauces and custards.

7 Semolina is formed when wheat grains are ground to make flour. Semolina can be cooked with milk to form a milk pudding.

BREAKFAST CEREALS made from Wheat, Maize, Oats, Rice

FLOUR made from Wheat

SEMOLINA made from Wheat

PEARL BARLEY made from Barley

CORNFLOUR made from Maize, (Corn)

OATMEAL made from Oats

SPAGHETTI, MACARONI made from Wheat

THE MAIN PRODUCTS FROM CEREALS

Some interesting facts about cereals

1 When Sir Walter Raleigh returned from his explorations of the part of America now known as Virginia, he brought back to England three plants which the English people had never seen before. They were potatoes, tobacco and ***maize.***

2 In China, the ***rice*** grain is still used in many religious ceremonies. Even in England the custom of throwing rice at a wedding continues.

3 In 1890 two brothers working in a wooden hut in Michigan (U.S.A.) began to experiment with ***wheat*** and discovered that it could be cooked and rolled into flakes to form a crisp and easily-digested food. This was the first breakfast cereal to be made and the two inventors were the Kellogg brothers.

4 It is believed that when the Pilgrim Fathers left England for the New World (America) they took with them some ***oats.*** This cereal grew so well in America that it has been grown there ever since.

Think and Do

1. Trace a map of the world into your notebooks. Shade in red one area where wheat is grown; shade in green one area where maize is grown; shade in yellow one area where rice is grown; and shade in blue one area where oats are grown. Don't forget to draw a key at the bottom of your map to show what each colour represents.

2. Copy this diagram into your books and supply the missing words:

The Food Value of Cereals

The h.......... contains vitamin.........

The germ contains vitamin........, some p.......... and fat.

The kernel contains large amounts of..........

3. Write the following sentences into your book using the correct word from the words in the brackets:

a. (Oats, Corn) is another name for maize.

b. Cornflour is made from (maize, wheat).

c. Oats are grown mainly in the (northern, southern) hemisphere.

d. (China, Peru) is a good rice-growing country.

e. Vitamin B is contained in the (kernel, germ) of the grain.

f. (Animal, Vegetable) protein is present in cereals in small amounts.

g. Maize was first introduced to this country by (Sir Walter Raleigh, Sir Francis Drake).

h. The Greek goddess of the harvest was called (Cerebos, Ceres).

i. (Rye, Rice) is grown in large quantities in Russia.

j. (Maize, Wheat) is the staple food of Great Britain.

4. Suggest a name for a new breakfast cereal which is to be made from oats. Design a suitable cover for the packet.

5. Oats, barley and wheat are the main cereal crops grown in England. Find out the month of the year when each of these crops is *a.* sown; *b.* harvested.

6. Suggest one dish that you could make using each of the following products:

a. wholemeal flour; *b.* pearl barley; *c.* medium oatmeal; *d.* semolina; *e.* white flour; *f.* macaroni; *g.* fine oatmeal; *h.* cornflour; *i.* spaghetti; *j.* a breakfast cereal.

7. Organize a competition in your class to see who can list the most names of breakfast cereals on sale in your local shops.

8. Plan a day's meals for a strict vegetarian and underline all the dishes which use cereals. Remember to include a good supply of vegetable protein.

9. What stories in the Bible have something to do with cereals?

10. Find out the current prices of each of the following:

a. 1 kg S.R. flour; *b.* 125 g packet of cornflour; *c.* 500 g rice; *d.* 500 g wholemeal flour; *e.* a small packet of laundry starch; *f.* 250 g pearl barley; *g.* 250 g fine oatmeal; *h.* a medium packet of porridge oats; *i.* a large white sliced loaf; *j.* a small packet of frozen sweet corn.

Chapter

13

How to store food wisely

One of the most important parts of cookery is to know how to store food wisely. The health of the entire household depends upon it, not to mention the saving of time and money in the kitchen.

Some foods do not store well. They quickly lose their freshness and go bad. Warning signs are if a mould starts to grow on the food or if there is a stale and unpleasant smell. Any food which has obviously gone bad must not be eaten. It should either be burned or wrapped in newspaper and put in the dustbin. Sometimes, however, food can go bad and yet it continues to look and smell all right. If the warning signs are missing, how then can you recognize food that is not fresh enough to be eaten? To be able to do this it is necessary to know what causes food to deteriorate and how you can prevent this happening.

How food becomes infected

Food is unfit to eat when it has become infected with **germs** or **bacteria.** These are present in the air around us. Food can become infected with germs and bacteria in several ways:

1 by **flies,** which may land on the food and pass on the dirt and disease which they carry;
2 by **dust** in the air;
3 by **human beings** who are not careful about their personal hygiene;
4 by **vermin** such as rats and mice;
5 by **pets** such as cats and dogs.

Date-stamping shows the shelf-life of perishable goods.

Foods which should be eaten within six weeks are labelled:

SELL BY + DAY + MONTH

Foods with a shelf-life of six weeks to twelve months (eighteen months after Jan. 1985) are labelled:

BEST BEFORE + MONTH + YEAR

How to prevent food from becoming infected

1 All food should be covered. Foods which keep well in storage tins or canisters are easily dealt with, but some foods require air in order to keep fresh (e.g. meat, cheese), and would smell musty and stale if kept in an airtight tin. These foods should be placed on a clean plate and covered with muslin. This will allow air to reach the food but will protect it from flies and dust.

2 Everybody who handles food must be clean enough to do so. Hands must be washed regularly and nails should be kept short and clean. Long, untidy nails provide a good hiding place for germs, so always check that your nails are a sensible length and look neat and clean.

Always use plenty of soap and hot water before handling food. This is particularly important after **each** visit to the toilet.

If you are handling food when you have a cough or a cold, do make sure that you cough or sneeze into a handkerchief, and not onto or near food. Remember that **'Coughs and sneezes spread diseases'**.

If you have any sores or blisters on your hands, or any other infection of the skin, do make sure that you cover your hands before handling food. A small plaster is often sufficient but rubber gloves can be worn if necessary.

3 All store cupboards and larders should be kept spotlessly clean. Dirty kitchens where unswept crumbs are left in the corners of the cupboards and floor, are an open invitation to mice, rats, and insects such as cockroaches. Don't let these unwelcome guests invade **your** home.

4 Pets should never be allowed near the family's food or the dining table. Cats and dogs can carry infection and disease on their paws and on the hair on their skin, so do discourage any member of the household from fondling them during mealtimes.

Some results of eating infected food

Bacteria and germs grow and multiply very quickly, and they are a constant source of danger to the health of one's family. Some bacteria can have hardly any effects on human beings but some can cause bad attacks of food poisoning. Fever, cramp, diarrhoea, bad headaches and sickness can all be caused by food poisoning, and it can even lead to death in serious cases.

How to prevent food poisoning
Because bacteria can have such unpleasant effects, care must be taken to stop the germs from multiplying. What can be done?

In *warm* surroundings germs will *multiply quickly.*
In *cold* surroundings germs will only *multiply very, very slowly.*
In *very hot* surroundings germs are *killed.*

Here we have the solution to our problem. If we store perishable food in a refrigerator where the air is very cold, then any germs which might be on the food will only be able to multiply very, very slowly. The chances of the food becoming so badly infected that it would be dangerous to eat, is considerably reduced. Always, therefore, keep food as *cool* as possible. This can be done by storing food in:
a a refrigerator;
b a well-ventilated larder with a cold slab;
c a cellar;
d a food safe in the open air, sheltered from sunshine.

Food such as joints of meat and cooked meat dishes should always be completely cooked through. It is important that the *inside* of the dish becomes *hot* enough to *kill* the germs which may be present. If a cooked joint of meat is left on the larder shelf, it may become re-infected with bacteria. If the joint is then warmed through, the bacteria will multiply in the warmth, making the meat dangerous to eat. If cooked meat is to be served hot it must be *completely* re-heated through.

Points to remember when storing food
1 All *perishable* foods should be bought fresh and used as quickly as possible. Meat should not be stored for longer than one day in a larder or three days in a refrigerator, before being cooked.

TO PREVENT THE SPREAD OF BACTERIA
(1) KEEP FOOD IN A COOL PLACE
(2) COOK FOOD THOROUGHLY
(3) KEEP COOKED FOOD IN A COOL PLACE
(4) IF NEEDED HOT, RE-HEAT COOKED FOOD THOROUGHLY

2 Fish should be cooked on the same day that it is bought.

3 Always keep *milk* cool. Milk will keep fresh for one day in a larder or two to three days in a refrigerator. Store it in a clean, covered jug.

4 Green vegetables keep best in the dark. Wrap them in a newspaper, or place them in a saucepan with a tightly-fitting lid. Salad ingredients will not keep fresh for longer than two to three days.

5 Root vegetables should be kept dry and in a vegetable rack so that air can circulate round them.

6 Fats such as butter, margarine and lard, should be kept cool in a larder or refrigerator.

7 Dry groceries, such as sugar and flour, should be stored in clean, airtight tins. Use them in the order that they are bought so that the new stock is put at the back of the larder and the old stock is used up first.

8 Frozen foods must be cooked immediately they have thawed. They can be stored whilst still frozen, in the ice-compartment of a refrigerator where they will keep for several weeks or even months. Freezers can be used for longer term storage of perishable foods.

Food hygiene in shops

It is important that food should be handled and stored properly in shops so that people do not buy food that has already become infected. Do be particular about the type of shop at which you buy your food. Here are some points that you can look for when you next go out shopping. See if you can suggest any others.

1 Shops should look clean, tidy and well-organized. Do be wary of any shop with untidy shelves or a dusty counter top.

2 Floor surfaces should be free from crumbs and look clean and well-polished.

3 Unwrapped foods such as whole cheeses and loose butter, should be covered with muslin or plastic lids.

4 Cooked meats and cakes should be handled with special plastic tongs which are kept for that particular food.

5 Shop assistants should have neat hairstyles so that hair does not flop onto food as they bend down.

6 Clean overalls should be worn by all assistants who handle

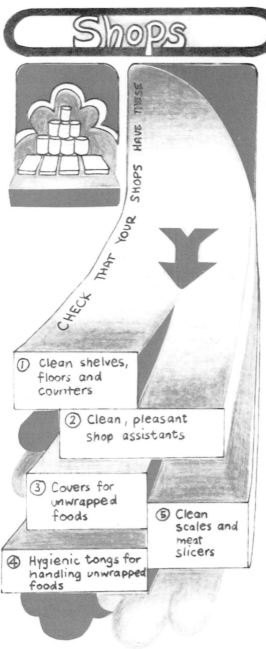

Shops

CHECK THAT YOUR SHOPS HAVE THESE

① Clean shelves, floors and counters

② Clean, pleasant shop assistants

③ Covers for unwrapped foods

④ Hygienic tongs for handling unwrapped foods

⑤ Clean scales and meat slicers

food and they should have clean hands and well-scrubbed nails.

7 Shopkeepers should politely discourage customers from taking pets into shops.

8 All food shops should display a NO SMOKING poster.

9 All scales and meat slicers should look spotlessly clean.

Cleanliness in the kitchen

1 All surfaces in the kitchen should be cleaned regularly, especially storage shelves and containers. Butter dishes and sugar bowls should be washed out at least once per week.

2 All food in the larder and in cupboards should be covered.

3 Sanibins should be emptied every day, washed and disinfected so that the germs are killed.

4 Dish cloths, tea towels and floor cloths should be regularly washed, boiled and disinfected.

5 Drains around the kitchen door and underneath window sills should be cleared of rubbish and bits of food and disinfectant poured down once per week.

6 Do not have the dustbin too near the kitchen door or window. In hot weather dustbins attract flies and insects which would quickly find their way into the kitchen.

7 Milk bottles should be washed immediately they are emptied and placed on the doorstep for the milkman to collect. To save this trouble a lot of milk is now sold in cartons.

8 All cooking utensils such as saucepans, scales and sieves should be cleaned thoroughly after use. Saucepans should not be stored with their lids on because this prevents air from circulating inside the saucepans and a musty, stale smell will result.

9 Any crumbs of food on the floor, or spilled liquids, should be mopped up immediately.

10 Do not allow family pets in the larder or near the surfaces on which you prepare food.

11 Always be very particular about your own personal hygiene when preparing meals for your family. Do you always look like this when you are working in the kitchen?

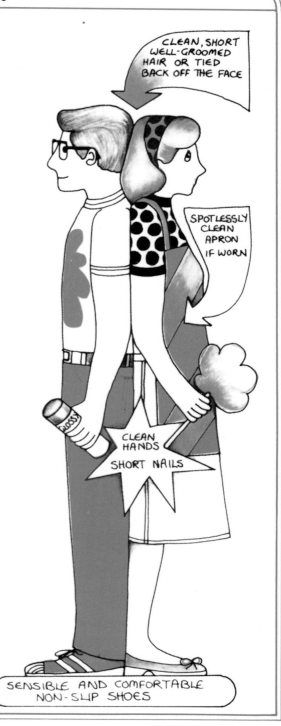

Ways of preserving food in the home

Fruits and other foods which do not keep fresh for long may be preserved. There are many different ways of doing this. Here are a few:

1. Making jams and marmalades
2. Bottling
3. Making fruit jellies
4. Making chutney
5. Pickling in vinegar
6. Preserving in salt
7. Drying
8. Freezing

Preserved foods keep well because the bacteria present have been destroyed or because the bacteria have not been allowed to multiply. These are the principles behind the preservation of food.

Bacteria are destroyed by extreme heat. This is what happens when making jams, marmalade, jellies, chutney, or bottling fruits. The bacteria are killed during cooking and the sealing of the jars prevents any other bacteria from entering and re-infecting the food.

Bacteria cannot multiply without moisture. In the drying of herbs, fruits and vegetables the moisture is removed so that the bacteria are unable to multiply.

Bacteria cannot multiply without warmth. In the freezing of foods, warmth is removed and this makes the bacteria harmless.

Some preserved foods keep fresh because a preservative has been added. Salt and vinegar are two preservatives which can be used as in the packing of vegetables in salt, and pickling in vinegar.

FREEZING FOOD AT HOME MEANS THAT

a. food can be bought in bulk at competitive prices;
b. fruit and vegetables can be bought in season when they are plentiful;
c. pre-prepared dishes can be stored to save time and energy at meal-times;
d. there is less wastage of food especially in times of glut;
e. there is a reserve of food to cater for the unexpected guest.

REMEMBER WHEN FREEZING FOOD!

1. Only good-quality food should be frozen.
2. Cooked food should be cooled thoroughly before being put in the freezer.
3. Food should be packed in suitable quantities to avoid wastage, and wrapped well in moisture-proof containers or polythene bags.
4. Packages of food should be labelled and dated.
5. Never re-freeze food which has been thawed.
6. The freezer lid or door should be kept closed and only opened when necessary.

Here is a summary of the main points about the preservation of foods:

---

1. Bacteria are killed by cooking at very high temperatures as in: *making jam, marmalade, fruit jellies, chutneys and bottling fruit*

---

2. Bacteria cannot grow when: *moisture has been removed, as in dried foods*
   warmth has been removed, as in frozen foods

---

3. Bacteria are killed by preservatives, as in: *pickling in vinegar*
   packing in salt

Think and Do

1. Design an outfit of clothes which you think would be **sensible** and **practical** for a person to wear, when working in the kitchen.

2. Arrange a 'Neatest Nails' competition with the rest of the class. Ask your housecraft teacher if she will judge who has the neatest and the most well-cared-for nails.

3. Walk through your local shopping centre and write a list of examples of bad hygiene that you can see in the display and handling of food.

4. Design a poster explaining the dangers of food poisoning and how it can be prevented.

5. Choose a word from List B to complete each of the sentences in List A. Write the complete sentences neatly into your books.

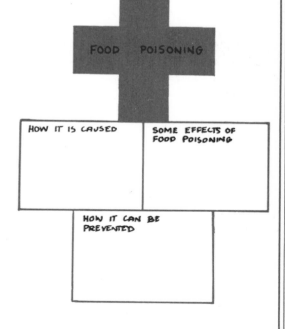

List A	List B
a. Food poisoning is caused by.................	*short*
b. Bacon should be covered with................. to keep it clean.	*mice*
c. ...., well-manicured nails are essential when handling food.	*warm*
d. In .... surroundings bacteria grow quickly.	*pets*
e. In very .... surroundings bacteria are killed.	*muslin*
f. .... should not be allowed near the table at mealtimes.	*refrigerator*
g. Crumbs of food on the floor will attract	*hot*
h. A .... can be used for storing perishable food.	*bacteria*

6. Copy the diagram into your notebooks and write a suitable sentence in each of the boxes. Colour the cross red.

7. Can you spot the dangers in this kitchen? In the picture there are eight possible sources of food poisoning. List them in your books.

8. List as many different ways as you can think of for preserving:

a. apples; *b.* tomatoes.

9. The following are well-known preserved foods in code. What are they?

a. LIPLALICI; *b.* MDOANS AMJ; *c.* TDBEOLT RESAP; *d.* NTEHYCU; *e.* IDEDR HRSBE; *f.* ICEDKLP GBAEBCA; *g.* ARLMEMDAA; *h.* TAESLD NESBA.

10. Are these sentences *true* or *false?*

a. Vinegar can be used for preserving some foods.

b. Bacteria are killed by freezing.

c. Milk should always be kept in an open jug so that fresh air can circulate around it.

d. Disinfectant should be poured down drains to kill germs.

e. When fruit is bottled, moisture is removed, and this helps the fruit to store well.

f. Food poisoning can be caused by flies.

g. Frozen foods must be cooked immediately they have thawed.

h. Long nails should be encouraged.

Part Three

All About Cooking

Chapter

14

Cooking methods

Why do we cook food? You should be able to suggest several answers to this question. The main reasons are, of course, that cooking is important because it:

a makes food more digestible;
b gives food added flavour;
c makes food look and smell more appetizing;
d makes some food safer to eat.

In this chapter we shall consider each of the different methods of cooking and see which foods are suitable for each method.

To cook food you must use **heat.** This can be supplied by using:

a hot fat (as in frying, roasting);
b hot water (as in boiling, stewing, steaming);
c dry heat (as in baking, grilling).

Cooking methods using hot fat

1 Frying. Frying is cooking food in hot fat. You can use either a small amount of fat, as in a frying pan, or a large amount of fat, as in a chip pan.

Foods, which are being fried, cook quickly, because the fat is so hot that the heat quickly reaches the inside of the food. This method is **not** suitable for cooking tough cuts of meat. It is important to remember that fat must be hot before you use it for frying. As fat is heated, it goes through **four** stages.

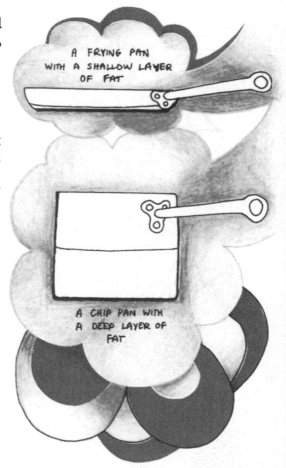

A FRYING PAN WITH A SHALLOW LAYER OF FAT

A CHIP PAN WITH A DEEP LAYER OF FAT

The fat is ready for frying when it reaches Stage 2, which is when a blue haze begins to rise from the fat. At this stage the heat should be turned down and the food to be cooked should be lowered gently into the hot fat.

All food to be fried must be dry. If wet food is placed into hot fat, the fat will spit and splash out fiercely. Most foods should be coated before being fried. Meat and potatoes already have a protective covering, but other foods should either be coated in egg and breadcrumbs or in a batter.

Foods which are suitable for frying

a All types of fish; *b* Steak, chops, sausages, bacon, liver; *c* Eggs, Scotch eggs, pancakes; *d* Fritters; *e* Doughnuts; *f* Potatoes.

2 Roasting. Roasting is cooking food in shallow, hot fat inside an oven. The food being cooked should be basted occasionally with the hot fat in order to keep it moist.

Foods suitable for roasting

a Tender joints of meat; *b* Poultry; *c* Potatoes.

Cooking methods using hot water

1 Boiling. Boiling means cooking food inside a boiling liquid. The liquid is usually water. Nutrients and flavour are often lost into the liquid during cooking but if the liquid can be used for making soups, sauces or stews, the goodness is not wasted. Boiling is a long, slow method of cooking food.

Foods suitable for boiling

a Vegetables; *b* Meat; *c* Eggs; *d* Macaroni, spaghetti, rice.

2 Stewing. Stewing is cooking food in a simmering liquid in a saucepan with a tightly-fitting lid or in a casserole inside the oven. The liquid is served with the food after cooking so there is no wastage of flavour or nutrients in stewed foods. Stewing is a long, slow method of cooking and will make even the tougher cuts of meat tender.

Foods suitable for stewing

a Fruit; *b* Tough cuts of meat; *c* Vegetables.

3 Steaming. Steaming is cooking food in the steam rising from boiling water. Special saucepans can be used for this method.

Food may also be steamed using an ordinary saucepan.

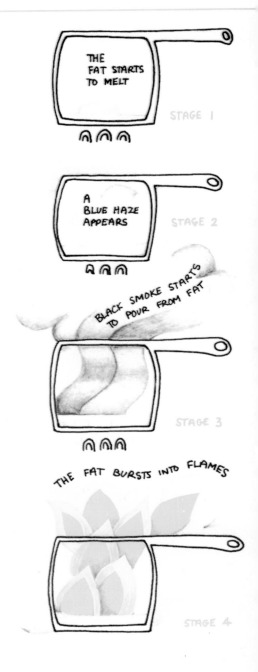

THE FAT STARTS TO MELT — STAGE 1

A BLUE HAZE APPEARS — STAGE 2

BLACK SMOKE STARTS TO POUR FROM FAT — STAGE 3

THE FAT BURSTS INTO FLAMES — STAGE 4

Steaming is a long, slow process. Steamed food is very digestible and is suitable for invalid dishes.

Foods suitable for steaming

a Fish; b Suet pastry puddings; c Vegetables; d Sponge puddings; e Tough cuts of meat (the meat must be cut up and cooked in pastry).

Cooking methods using dry heat

1 Baking. Baking is cooking food in the dry heat inside an oven. Baked foods usually have a good colour and flavour.

Foods suitable for baking

a Cakes and puddings; b Fish; c Pastry dishes; d Bread; e Potatoes; f Meat.

2 Grilling. Grilling is cooking food underneath an intense source of heat. There is a grill compartment to all modern cookers. Grilling is a very quick method of cooking food. It is not suitable for tough cuts of meat.

Foods suitable for grilling

a Tender cuts of meat (chops, steak, kidney, liver, sausage); b Mushrooms; c Tomatoes; d Fish.

Other methods

There are two other methods of cooking which have not yet been mentioned and do not belong to any of the groups we have already mentioned. They are *braising* and *pressure cooking.*

Braising is another method for cooking *meat.* It is a mixture of frying, steaming and stewing. A selection of vegetables is fried and then placed in the bottom of a casserole dish. The joint of meat is then placed on top of the vegetables and a little water is added. The dish is covered and cooked slowly inside an oven.

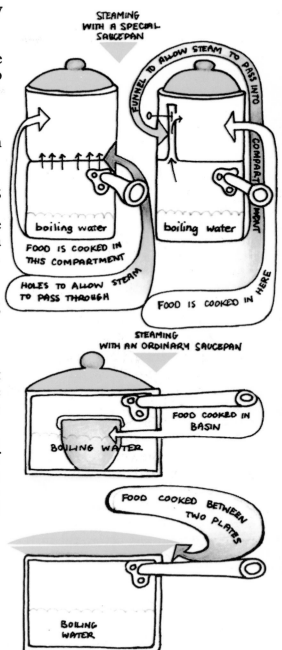

STEAMING WITH A SPECIAL SAUCEPAN

FUNNEL TO ALLOW STEAM TO PASS INTO COMPARTMENT

boiling water

boiling water

FOOD IS COOKED IN THIS COMPARTMENT

HOLES TO ALLOW STEAM TO PASS THROUGH

FOOD IS COOKED IN HERE

STEAMING WITH AN ORDINARY SAUCEPAN

FOOD COOKED IN BASIN

BOILING WATER

FOOD COOKED BETWEEN TWO PLATES

BOILING WATER

LID

MEAT

VEGETABLES

WATER

Pressure cooking is cooking food in an increased pressure inside a special container or saucepan. Water normally boils at 100°C but if the pressure can be decreased the water will boil at a lower temperature. If the pressure is increased the water will boil at a higher temperature. This is what happens inside a pressure cooker: ◀☞

Automatically-controlled ovens

Many modern ovens have complicated-looking dials and knobs at the top. These are for use if you need to go out for a while but want the meal to be ready when you get back. By reading the instructions with the cooker you can pre-set the dials so that the cooker will:

1 Switch itself on;

2 Heat itself to the right temperature;

3 Cook for the right length of time;

4 Switch itself off.

This type of oven is obviously a great help to a busy person.

Cooking in aluminium foil

Aluminium foil is another modern kitchen aid. It has many uses. It can be used for:

1 Covering dishes which are to be baked, steamed or casseroled;

2 Wrapping up foods to be taken on a picnic;

3 Lining cake tins;

4 Completely wrapping around fish, joints of meat and poultry before they are baked.

The foil stops heat escaping during cooking and so the dish cooks quickly. The food does not shrink as much as it does during open baking, and there is no loss of flavour or nutrients from the food. If a better colour is needed the foil can be removed just before the dish is cooked through and this will allow the food to brown.

Microwave cookers

Originally used by caterers for cooking meals quickly, these are now in many homes. The food is heated by microwaves and is cooked very quickly but not all foods are suitable. Quick defrosting of frozen foods is also possible.

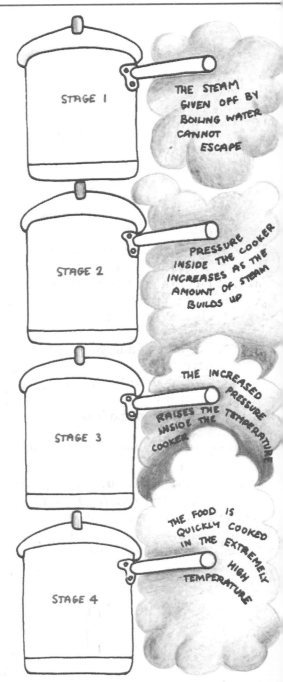

STAGE 1

THE STEAM GIVEN OFF BY BOILING WATER CANNOT ESCAPE

STAGE 2

PRESSURE INSIDE THE COOKER INCREASES AS THE AMOUNT OF STEAM BUILDS UP

STAGE 3

THE INCREASED PRESSURE RAISES THE TEMPERATURE INSIDE THE COOKER

STAGE 4

THE FOOD IS QUICKLY COOKED IN THE EXTREMELY HIGH TEMPERATURE

Think and Do

1. Trace or draw this diagram into your books, and complete the sentences in each of the boxes.

2. The following is a mixed grill. Of what does it consist?

CNABO   LITFEL EKSTA
UGAESSA   MTATOO
NDYIKE   LVREI
ROSUMOHM

3. Suggest some suitable picnic dishes which can be wrapped in aluminium foil to keep hot.

4. Complete the following crossword in your notebook:

Clues across
1. Do this occasionally when roasting
2. For all cooking you need this
3. Can be used for lining cake tins
4. Comes from boiling water

Clues down
1. A coating
5. Can be used when stewing

5. Suggest a suitable way of cooking each of the following dishes or foods:
a. an invalid dish; *b.* a cheap cut of meat; *c.* potatoes; *d.* fish; *e.* tomatoes; *f.* sausage; *g.* rump steak; *h.* a suet pudding; *i.* fritters; *j.* a chicken.

6. Have a good look at a modern electric cooker that has an automatic timer for the oven. ***Read the instructions carefully*** and then see if you can set the dials to give each of the following:
a. After 3 hours delay—heat, up to 220°C for $\frac{3}{4}$ hour.
b. After 5 hours delay—heat, up to 180°C for 2 hours.
c. After 7 hours delay—heat, up to 200°C for 4 hours.

7. Choose a word from Column B to complete each sentence in Column A. Write the completed sentences into your notebook.

METHODS OF COOKING FOOD

This is a hot plate On it we can steam, f.......... or s.......... food.

This is the grill. With this we can g.......... food.

This is the oven. In here we can r........, s........, or casserole.

Column A

Column B

a. Stewing is an .... method of cooking food.

best

b. Baking is cooking food in .... heat in an enclosed space.

digestible

c. Steamed food is more .... than food cooked by other methods.

dry

d. Fish must be .... before being fried to prevent the flakes from falling apart.

slow

e. During boiling there is often a loss of .... into the cooking water.

economical

f. Steaming is cooking food in the heat rising from .... water.

coated

g. Grilling is only suitable for .... quality meat.

boiling

h. ...., steady cooking is required when stewing.

nutrients

8. Draw a diagram in your notebook showing how you would steam a steak and kidney pudding if you did not have a proper steamer. Underneath your diagram explain how the food is cooked.

9. Make a list of all the different methods of cooking food and opposite each method write four dishes which could be suitably cooked in that way, e.g.

steaming—fish, steak and kidney pudding, jam layer pudding, jam roly-poly.

10. Copy the following diagram into your notebook and write a suitable sentence in each of the boxes.

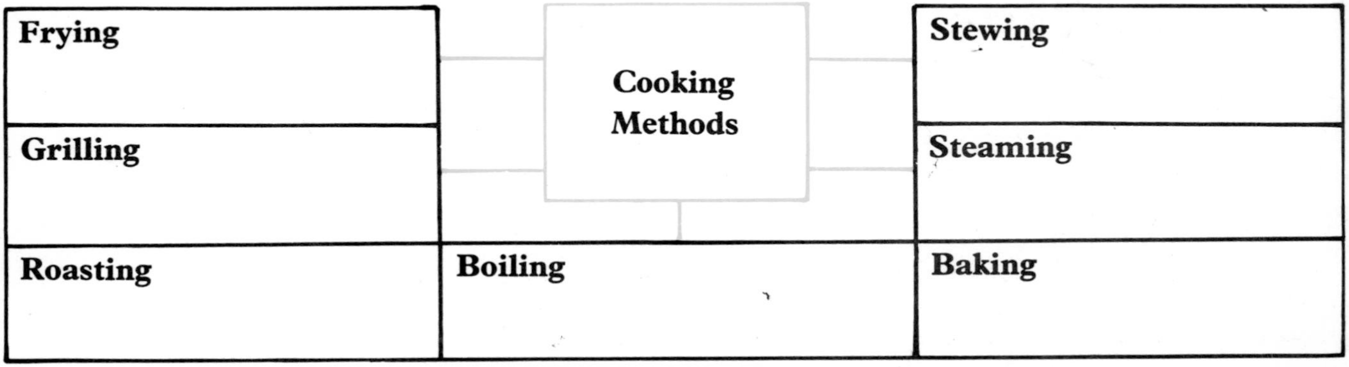

Frying		Stewing
Grilling	Cooking Methods	Steaming
Roasting	Boiling	Baking

Chapter

15

Understanding recipes

When you next pick up a magazine turn to the cookery section and read carefully through the recipes that are given. You should find that each recipe is a complete description of how to make the dish concerned. It should give details of how to **prepare** and **cook** the dish. Each recipe should tell you four main points:

1 The ingredients which are to be used.
2 The amounts of ingredients needed.
3 How the dish is prepared.
4 How the dish is cooked.

Always read through a recipe carefully and check **before you start to make a dish** that:

1 You have the right ingredients and equipment;
2 You have sufficient of each ingredient;
3 You have enough time to prepare and cook the dish.

Planning your work

Plan your work carefully. Always know exactly what dishes you are going to prepare before you start and in what order you are going to make them. Try to save time where this is possible. For example, if you are baking two dishes needing short crust pastry, just make one large amount of pastry and divide it between the two dishes.

Collect together the ingredients you need and check with the recipe to see if there are any utensils you must prepare. For example, cake tins may have to be greased and lined and as this is a messy job tackle it before you have to handle any food.

Using the oven

If you will be needing the oven for your cookery see that it is switched on before you begin. All electric and gas cookers have a numbered dial on the outside of the oven. This is called the **Gas Mark** or (on some older cookers) **Regulo** and it controls the amount of heat inside the oven. A low number will give a cool oven whereas a high number will give a hot oven.

The gas marks on gas cookers are numbered from $\frac{1}{4}$ to 9. This means that numbers below 2 are cool; numbers 3 and 4 are warm; 5 and 6 are moderately hot; 7 is hot and 8 and 9 are very hot.

Modern electric cookers are numbered as degrees in the Celsius scale. The main divisions are at 50°C intervals, and range from 100°C to 250°C. Smaller marks will indicate 10°C intervals. This means that up to 150°C will give a cool oven; from 170°C to 180°C will be warm; from 190°C to 200°C will be moderately hot; from 220°C will be hot and from 230°C will be very hot.

Older cookers may be numbered in the Fahrenheit scale, but the conversion to °C is shown on page 107.

Your recipe will tell you which heat you require. Set the dial in the correct position immediately you have lit the oven. The chart on the page opposite will help you remember the oven heats for some simple dishes.

The position of shelves. The shelves inside the oven may need to be moved if they are not in the correct position. **Do this while the oven is still cool.** Some dishes cook better at the top of the oven, some in the middle of the oven and a few in the bottom. Here is a guide to help you position your shelves properly:

A fan heated oven gives an even heat, so when using this type of oven the positioning of dishes is not important. Always check that cakes and bread mixtures have room in which to rise.

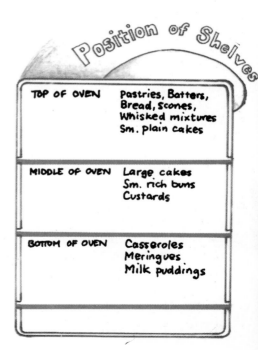

Position of Shelves

TOP OF OVEN	Pastries, Batters, Bread, Scones, Whisked mixtures Sm. plain cakes
MIDDLE OF OVEN	Large cakes Sm. rich buns Custards
BOTTOM OF OVEN	Casseroles Meringues Milk puddings

Dish	Gas	Electric	
		Celsius	Fahrenheit
Meringues	2	150°	300°
Large rich fruit cakes **Milk puddings** **Egg custards**	3	170°	325°
Biscuits **Small rich buns** **Victoria sandwich**	4	180°	350°
Casseroles	5	190°	375°
Roasted meat **Baked fish**	6	200°	400°
Short crust pastry **Scones** **Batters** **Rock and raspberry buns** **Flaky pastry**	7	220°	425°
Whisked mixtures **Bread**	8	230°	450°

Measuring your ingredients
How to use scales. Your next job is to weigh your ingredients accurately. You must be careful when weighing because too much flour or too little fat can ruin a mixture. **Weigh carefully and accurately every time.**

There are three types of kitchen scales:
1 The dial scale;
2 The horizontal bar scale;
3 The balancing scale.

All about cooking

When using a **_dial scale_** place the ingredients you are weighing in the scale pan until the finger on the front dial points to the exact weight you are needing.

When using a **_horizontal bar scale_** place the ingredients you are weighing on the scale pan until the finger moves along the bar and points to the weight you are needing.

When using a **_balancing scale_** place the weight on the small scale pan and the ingredients you are weighing on the large pan. The scales should balance evenly for the correct weight. If either side goes down with a thud, your ingredients are not being weighed accurately.

Measuring solids. In the metric system solids are weighed in **grams** and **kilograms**. There are 1000 grams in a kilogram and 500 grams in ½ kilogram. Dial and horizontal bar scales are marked at 25 gram intervals. Balancing scales have loose metric weights starting at 25 grams.

The 250 g blocks of fat are relatively easy to divide into 25 g cubes without the use of a scale. This can be done by cutting the block into 10 equal sections. If you use your ruler to mark the outside of the wrapper it will help you.

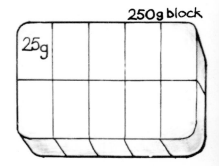

Measuring using spoons. Special measuring spoons, often square for easy levelling, can be bought in the following sizes: 1·25 ml; 2·5 ml; 5 ml; 10 ml; 15 ml; 20 ml. If these special measuring spoons are not available a 5 ml 'medicine' spoon can be used.

A spoonful of any dry ingredient means a **rounded** spoonful (as much above the rim as below it).

Half a spoonful means a **levelled** spoonful (level with the rim of the spoon).

A quarter of a spoonful means **half of a levelled** spoonful.

If a recipe requires 1 × 5 ml spoon baking powder, then this means a rounded 5 ml spoonful of baking powder.

If a recipe requires ½ × 5 ml spoon salt, then this means a levelled 5 ml spoonful of salt.

If a recipe requires ¼ × 5 ml spoon dried herbs, then this means half of a levelled spoonful of dried herbs.

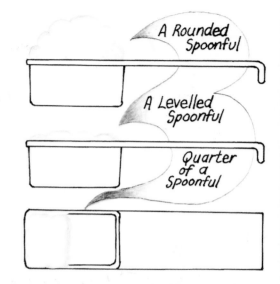

Measuring using cups. If you do not have a pair of metric scales you can still measure fairly accurately using measuring cups. These measures are available in the following sizes:

Measuring liquids. In the metric system, liquids are measured in millilitres, centilitres, decilitres and litres. There are:

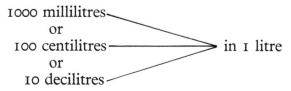

1000 millilitres
or
100 centilitres — in 1 litre
or
10 decilitres

When measuring liquids, special jugs can be used which have a scale down one side. These jugs are called measuring

jugs or measures. Measuring jugs can be obtained in 1 litre and 500 millilitre sizes. The 1 litre size is marked at intervals of 7·5 dl, 5 dl, 1·25 dl and 1 dl. The 500 millilitre size is marked at intervals of 2·5 dl, 1·25 dl and 1 dl. If a recipe requires 500 millilitres liquid, either: *a* fill a 500 millilitre jug to the correct level or *b* half fill a litre measuring jug to the 5 decilitre level.

When measuring small quantities of liquid, the 5 ml, 10 ml and 20 ml spoons already described can be used.

Abbreviations in recipes

Here is a list of shortened words (or abbreviations) which are often used in recipes.

g	= gram
kg	= kilogram
l	= litre
ml	= millilitre
cl	= centilitre
dl	= decilitre
S.R.	= self-raising (flour)
temp.	= temperature
C	= Celsius

Cookery terms

When you have measured your ingredients correctly you are ready to begin cooking. Here are some cookery terms which you will find in recipes and may not understand.

basting	spooning liquid over food during cooking to keep it moist.
beating	getting air into a mixture by continually lifting it with a spoon.
blending	gradually adding a liquid to a powder to form a smooth mixture.
bouquet-garni	a selection of herbs which are tied together in muslin and dropped into soups and casseroles to add flavour.

coating	covering foods with a protective layer before frying or serving. Can be egg and breadcrumbs, a batter or a sauce.
creaming	mixing fat and sugar together until it is white and fluffy.
folding	very carefully adding a dry ingredient to a moist mixture, e.g. flour to softened fat, sugar and eggs in a creamed cake mixture.
garnishing	decorating dishes with colourful tit-bits of food.
glazing	brushing over uncooked pastry dishes with beaten egg, milk or a syrup to give them a glossy finish, or brushing over meat and fish dishes with a jelly (aspic) to improve their taste and appearance.
kneading	working a mixture into the correct shape and consistency using the knuckles and palms of the hands.
raising agent	an ingredient which when added to cakes, bread and pastries makes them rise, e.g. baking powder, yeast and bicarbonate of soda.
roux	a paste formed by mixing flour and melted fat. It is the first stage in making a sauce.
rubbing-in	lightly mixing in fat to flour using the fingertips.
seasoning	adding flavour and taste to foods by using salt and pepper, herbs (e.g. sage, parsley, thyme) or spices (e.g. cinnamon, nutmeg, curry powder).
simmering	cooking in a liquid that is just below boiling point.
whisking	beating air into ingredients (e.g. whisking eggs and sugar for a cake mixture, whisking egg whites for a meringue mixture).

Testing to see if foods are cooked

When the dish has been prepared always check with your recipe to see for how long your dish needs to be cooked. An approximate time will be given but this should only be treated as a guide. If a dish requires 15 minutes at gas mark 7 or 220°C, do not bring it out of the oven after 15 minutes unless it **looks** completely cooked. Use your own common sense to decide whether or not your dish is cooked through. Here are some points to look for when deciding whether food is cooked or not.

Dish	Appearance when cooked
Short crust and flaky pastries	Will look golden brown in colour. Should be firm to the touch. Pastry should be brown underneath. Filling should be soft.
Small, plain cakes	Will look golden brown in colour. Should be firm to the touch. Should be brown underneath.
Small, rich cakes	Will spring back when lightly touched in the middle. Should be golden brown in colour.
Large cakes	Should be firm to the touch. Golden brown in colour. When pierced with a warmed knitting needle or skewer no mixture should be sticking to the point of the needle or skewer when removed.
Joints of meat	Should look cooked. Should be tender when tested with a skewer or fork.
Fish	Should flake easily off the bone and skin. Should have a watery liquid escaping.

Think and Do

1. Select any four recipes from magazines. Stick them into your books and underneath each one write: *a.* at what position in the oven you would cook the dish; *b.* how you would tell when the dish was completely cooked.

2. Choose a simple dish that you have made at school. Write the recipe briefly in your own words, including all the main points.

3. At what oven heat would you bake each of the following dishes:

a. jam tarts; *b.* Victoria sandwich; *c.* egg custard; *d.* tea-cakes; *e.* lemon meringue pie; *f.* Christmas cake; *g.* a chicken; *h.* Swiss roll; *i.* hotpot; *j.* sausage rolls.

4. Calculate how many:

a. decilitres in $\frac{1}{2}$ litre; *b.* millilitres in $\frac{1}{4}$ litre; *c.* centilitres in $\frac{3}{4}$ litre; *d.* grams in $1\frac{1}{2}$ kilograms; *e.* 5 millilitre spoonfuls in 1 litre.

5. Complete the following crossword:

Clues across

1. There are one thousand of these in a kilogram
2. The scale now used on an electric oven thermostat
3. A measure for liquids

Clues down

4. The gas mark needed when baking scones
5. A herb
6. A paste formed by mixing flour and melted fat

6. Are these sentences *true* or *false*?

a. There are 1000 millilitres in 1 litre.

b. A levelled spoonful is equivalent to half a spoonful.

c. There are 500 grams in 1 kilogram.

d. Shortcrust pastry needs a cool oven.

e. Gas mark 7 is equal to 220°C.

f. To test if large cakes are cooked, pierce with a cold skewer.

g. Meringues should be cooked in a hot oven.

h. Simmering is cooking in a liquid that is just below boiling point.

i. Milk puddings should be cooked at the top of the oven.

j. A litre is equal to 10 decilitres.

7. Imagine you have the following ingredients available in your larder: a swiss roll, a pint of milk; sugar; blancmange powders; glacé cherries and a tin of fruit salad. Make up a simple recipe for a cold sweet using any or all of these items.

8. Using flour as a guide see *a.* how many 5 ml spoonfuls, and *b.* how many 10 ml spoonfuls will equal 50 g. Write your findings neatly into your book.

9. Have fun in working out the metric sizes of the following items of ovenware. Convert inch sizes to the nearest whole centimetre, e.g. A 6 inch sandwich tin (15·2 cm) will become 15 cm.

a. a swiss roll tin; *b.* an 8 inch cake tin; *c.* a small fluted pastry cutter; *d.* a 7 inch pie dish; *e.* a baking sheet; *f.* a savoury flan ring.

10. Plan a complete lunch that you could cook using the inside of the oven.

Chapter 16

Raising agents

In this chapter we are going to learn about different raising agents and how to use them properly in cookery.

Raising agents are added to cakes and some pastries. As the name suggests raising agents are used in cookery to make ingredients rise. It is the raising agent in a mixture that is responsible for pushing up the flour during cooking, so that the finished result will:

1 look appetising;
2 taste spongy and light;
3 be easy to digest.

Here is a list of the more common raising agents which you can use in your cooking.

---

1 **baking powder** 2 **self-raising flour** 3 **bicarbonate of soda** 4 **bicarbonate of soda with cream of tartar**	These are called **chemical** raising agents because they are made from **chemicals**

---

5 **air** 6 **yeast**	These are called **natural** raising agents because they are present in **nature** and are not manufactured

---

How raising agents work

All raising agents work in the same way. Imagine that you are baking a fruit cake. This is what will happen inside the cake as it cooks.

1 When the raising agent (baking powder) is mixed with moisture (the egg and milk) and then heated (as the cake cooks) it will give off a gas.

Raising agent + Moisture + Heat → GAS

2 This gas will get hotter and hotter as the cake cooks, and the heat will make the gas grow bigger (expand).

3 As the gas expands it will push up the flour in the cake. (The flour has already been softened by the moisture and so it will stretch like elastic.)

4 The heat of the oven will then cook the cake in this 'stretched' position.

5 Having done its work, the gas will escape. You are therefore left with a light and well-risen fruit cake.

Now let us consider each raising agent in more detail.

1. GAS IS FORMED INSIDE THE CAKE

2. GAS EXPANDS WITH THE HEAT

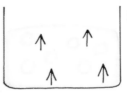

3. EXPANDED GAS STRETCHES THE FLOUR AND THE CAKE RISES

4. HEAT OF OVEN BAKES THE CAKE IN THIS RISEN POSITION

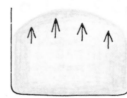

5. THE GAS ESCAPES

1 Baking powder

Baking powder is a white powder which can be added to plain flour when making cakes and some pastries. Baking powder is made from a mixture of bicarbonate of soda and an acid. When baking powder is used in cookery the gas given off is called **carbon dioxide.**

Baking powder	+ Heat	+ Moisture	→ GAS
(Bicarbonate of soda and an acid)	(in oven)	(in cake mixture)	(Carbon Dioxide)

Points to remember when using baking powder

a Always keep baking powder in an airtight tin, and do not try to store it for any length of time.

b When adding baking powder to a mixture, sieve it with the flour. This mixes the raising agent and the flour thoroughly.

c Use the correct amount of baking powder for the cakes being made.

Amount of baking powder (in 5 ml spoons) used with 500 g plain flour	
Scone mixtures	3–4
Plain cakes	2–3
Rich cakes	1
Suet pastry	2

2 Self-raising flour

Self-raising flour is flour which has had a chemical raising agent added to it during manufacture. The gas formed when self-raising flour is used in cakes is **carbon dioxide.**

3 Bicarbonate of soda

Bicarbonate of soda can be used by itself as a raising agent. When it is heated **carbon dioxide** is given off. Bicarbonate of soda has some disadvantages.

It leaves a very unpleasant taste in cakes. When carbon dioxide is formed, the bicarbonate of soda is turned into **washing soda** which obviously leaves a peculiar taste in cakes. A cure for this is to use bicarbonate of soda with a strongly-flavoured food such as vinegar or treacle. This then hides the unpleasant taste from the washing soda.

Bicarbonate of soda + Heat + Moisture → Carbon Dioxide and Washing Soda

Bicarbonate of soda has a 'yellowing' effect on cakes. This is not harmful but it does spoil the appearance of cakes. In darkly-coloured cakes (e.g. parkin) this effect is not noticed.

Points to remember when using bicarbonate of soda

a Only use this raising agent when making strongly-flavoured and darkly-coloured cakes.

b Always store bicarbonate of soda (and other chemical raising agents as well) in an airtight tin or container.

4 Bicarbonate of soda and cream of tartar

A mixture of bicarbonate of soda and cream of tartar may be used in cake-making. The acid (cream of tartar) prevents the bicarbonate of soda being turned into washing soda. The gas given off is **carbon dioxide.**

Bicarbonate of soda + Cream of tartar + Heat + Moisture → Carbon Dioxide

Points to remember when using bicarbonate of soda and cream of tartar

a Always use the correct amounts. For 500 g plain flour use 1 × 5 ml spoon of bicarbonate of soda and 2 × 5 ml spoons of cream of tartar.

b When making scones with sour milk, use only half the amount of cream of tartar (i.e. for 500 g plain flour use 1 × 5 ml spoon of bicarbonate of soda and 1 × 5 ml spoon of cream of tartar). This will allow for the acid present in sour milk.

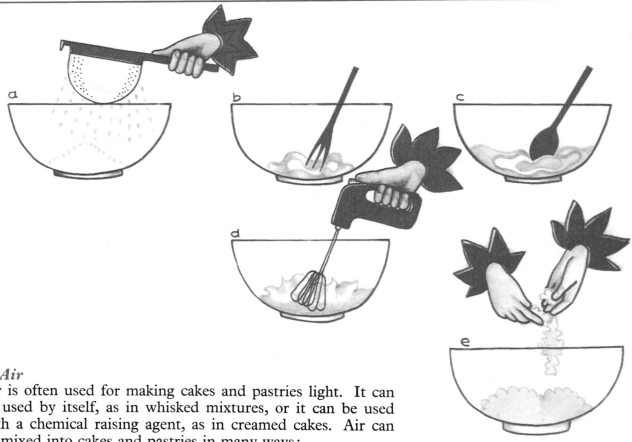

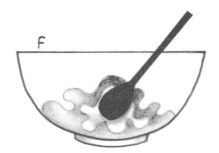

5 Air

Air is often used for making cakes and pastries light. It can be used by itself, as in whisked mixtures, or it can be used with a chemical raising agent, as in creamed cakes. Air can be mixed into cakes and pastries in many ways:

a· by sieving the flour and salt together;

b by beating the eggs lightly with a fork before adding them to a mixture;

c by creaming fat and sugar, and beating in eggs into a mixture;

d by whisking egg whites until they are stiff and full of air, and then lightly folding them into a mixture;

e by handling lightly and lifting up the mixture when rubbing fat into flour;

f by beating well when making batters.

Remember that when using air as a raising agent, flour should be folded in lightly. A mixture that is stirred or moved harshly will lose air, and so there will be less raising agent left to make the cake light.

6 Yeast

Yeast is the raising agent used in bread-making. Bread which is made without yeast is called **unleavened** bread. Can you think of any story in the Bible where reference is made to unleavened bread?

Fresh yeast is a living plant, which requires the same conditions as the green plants in your garden in order to stay alive. Yeast needs:

a warmth;

b moisture (water, milk or eggs);

c food (sugar).

When yeast is supplied with these three items the gas called **carbon dioxide** is given off and this makes the bread rise.

Yeast + Warmth + Moisture + Food → Carbon Dioxide

Yeast is killed by very hot temperatures. When bread is baked in a hot oven, the heat kills the yeast as it bakes the bread. Carbon dioxide cannot be given off by dead yeast and so the bread stops rising. Yeast can be bought as fresh yeast or dried yeast.

Points to remember when using yeast

a Always keep yeast in a warm atmosphere but not in a hot one. Why?

b Use the correct amount of yeast (i.e. for 500 g plain flour use 10 g yeast; for $1\frac{1}{2}$ kg plain flour use 25 g yeast).

There is one more raising agent which we have not yet mentioned. Can you think what it might be?

When cooking mixtures which have a large amount of liquid (e.g. batters) **steam** is the raising agent. The heat of the oven makes the liquid boil and so give off steam, which then pushes up the flour and makes the mixture rise. Steam can only be a raising agent where there is:

1 a large amount of liquid;

2 a very hot oven for baking.

We have now discussed each raising agent in turn and you will be able to choose for yourself which you prefer to use. What do you think are the advantages of using self-raising flour over plain flour with baking powder?

Think and Do

1. Name a suitable raising agent for each of the following dishes:
a. Swiss roll; *b.* suet dumplings; *c.* scones; *d.* Chelsea buns; *e.* gingerbread; *f.* jam tarts; *g.* Victoria sandwich; *h.* tea cakes; *i.* Yorkshire puddings; *j.* rock buns.

2. Copy the following diagram into your notebooks and supply the missing words:

RAISING AGENTS CAN BE DIVIDED INTO 2 GROUPS:	HERE ARE SOME RAISING AGENTS
1 NATURAL eg. air and	1 Self..............flour 2 .... powder
2 .... eg. baking powder	3 Bicarb. of .... 4 Bicarb. of ....and .... of tartar 5 Air 6 Yeast

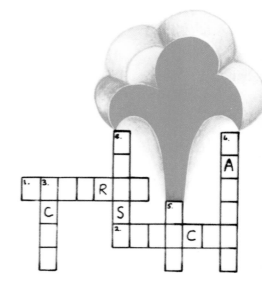

3. Solve the crossword shown.

4. Complete the following sentences using the correct word from the alternatives given in the brackets:

a. (Carbon monoxide, Carbon dioxide, Hydrogen) is the gas given off when baking powder is added to cakes.

b. Self-raising flour has been treated during manufacture and (yeast, tartaric acid, baking powder) has been added.

c. When bicarbonate of soda is used as a raising agent a flavour of (washing soda, carbolic, sodium chloride) remains in the cake.

d. Yeast is a living (powder, flower, plant) which is used in bread-making.

e. Yeast requires three items in order to stay alive—warmth, moisture and (food, sunshine, currants).

Clues across
1. Group of raising agents
2. Can be used to hide taste of washing soda

Clues down
3. Present in sour milk
4. Helps bread to rise
5. Given off by raising agents.
6. Steam is the raising agent in this

f. Air can be trapped inside pastry by (using a metal spoon, adding cold water, sieving the flour and salt).

5. List as many different kinds of loaves as you can think of. In what other shapes can dough be baked?

6. Find as many stories in the Bible as you can in which leavened and unleavened bread are mentioned.

7. Buy a little fresh yeast and *a.* look at it; *b.* touch it, and *c.* taste it. In your notebook, and under the heading 'Yeast—a living plant', describe what you noticed when looking, touching and tasting the yeast.

8. Collect three flasks (or small bottles) and three balloons. Cream together 25 g yeast and 2×5 ml spoons of sugar. Divide the creamed yeast equally amongst the three bottles, and pour in.

Label one 'Bottle A' and add $\frac{1}{2}$ pint *cold* water. Place a balloon over the neck of the bottle. Label the next one 'Bottle B' and add $\frac{1}{2}$ pint *warm* water. Place a balloon over the neck of the bottle. Label the third bottle 'Bottle C' and add $\frac{1}{2}$ pint *boiling* water. Place a balloon over the neck of the bottle.

Describe in your notebook the appearance of each of the balloons after *a.* $\frac{1}{2}$ hour; *b.* 2 hours. What has happened to give these results?

9. Imagine that a packet of flour has lost its label, and you cannot decide whether it is plain or self-raising flour. Experiment using ordinary household equipment, and try to find an easy method of telling the difference.

10. Describe in your own words how you could:

a. kill yeast;

b. include air in short crust pastry;

c. use sour milk for making scones;

d. hide the unpleasant taste when using bicarbonate of soda.

11. Copy the following paragraph into your books and supply the missing words.

'There are two groups of raising agents:

a. .... raising agents (e.g. air and ....).

b. Chemical raising agents (e.g. .... and ....).
When baking powder is mixed with moisture and ...., the gas called .... is given off, and this makes cakes rise.'

Chapter 17

Making pastry

Now we shall learn about the different methods of making pastry and how the common faults in pastry-making can be avoided.

Food value of pastry dishes

All pastries are made from **flour** and **fat.** They are therefore rich in **carbohydrates** (starch) and **fat,** and provide energy for work and heat. Pastries are usually baked as shells or cases for other foods, so when considering the food value of any pastry dish we must also consider the filling. For example, bacon and egg flan contains:

Starch **Fat**	in pastry
Protein **Fat**	in filling
Vitamins **Mineral salts** **Water**	also present in eggs, bacon, fat. seasoning, etc.

The different kinds of pastry

There are many different kinds of pastry. Those most commonly used in cookery are:

1 short crust; *2* suet; *3* flaky; *4* rough puff.

All pastries contain flour, fat and a liquid. The liquid is usually water but egg can also be used for some pastries. The amount of fat to use depends on the type of pastry being made.

Type of pastry	Proportion fat to flour	*Example*
1 Short crust	$\frac{1}{2}$	*For 200 g flour use 100 g fat*
2 Suet	$\frac{1}{3}$ to $\frac{1}{2}$	*For 200 g flour use 75–100 g fat*
3 Flaky	$\frac{3}{4}$	*For 200 g flour use 150 g fat*
4 Rough puff	$\frac{3}{4}$	*For 200 g flour use 150 g fat*

How are you to know how much pastry you will require for the dish you are making? Look at the recipe. If it states 'Make 100 g short crust pastry' then it means that you must use 100 g flour to make the pastry. Amounts of pastry **always** refer to the amount of flour required. For example, 'Make 200 g short crust pastry' means use 200 g flour and 100 g fat. (You will also notice that by remembering the proportion of fat to flour for short crust pastry we have been able to calculate that 100 g fat are also needed.)

Remember that if you are using the same pastry for more than one dish it will save time and energy if you make one large quantity of pastry and divide it amongst the dishes.

How to make light pastry
In the previous chapter we learned about raising agents. Can you remember the name of the raising agent in pastry? It is **air,** isn't it, that makes pastry light? There are several ways of trapping air into a mixture.

1 Sieve together the flour and salt. As the mixture falls back into the bowl, air will be trapped inside.

2 When the fat is rubbed into the flour, lift the mixture up out of the bowl, and always handle it very lightly.

3 When making flaky and rough puff pastries, air is trapped between the layers of pastry as it is being folded.

4 Suet pastry is different from the other three pastries because a chemical raising agent is used. A small amount of baking powder is added to the mixture.

Type of pastry	Raising agent
1 **Short crust**	air
2 **Suet**	baking powder
3 **Flaky**	air
4 **Rough puff**	air

Remember that raising agents work by expanding as a result of the heat in the oven. If a mixture is very cold when it is put into a hot oven, the gas inside the mixture will expand far more than if the mixture had been warm. In pastry-making, therefore, we must aim to keep the mixture as cool as possible so that the gases will expand properly and make the pastry light.

How to keep pastry cool
1 Use flour that has been stored in a **cool, dry** place.
2 Rub the fat into the flour with the **fingertips,** because these are the coolest parts of your hands.
3 Add **cold** water.
4 Stir the water in with a **metal** knife.
5 Handle the pastry **as little as possible.**
6 Leave the pastry in a **cool** place for a few minutes before using. This is particularly important when making flaky and rough puff pastries.

Now let us learn how each of the different pastries is made.

1 Short crust pastry
This is easily the most popular pastry. It can be used for sweet and savoury dishes, for puddings, tarts, pies, flans and pasties. As its name suggests short crust pastry should be

'short' in texture and crumbly and light to eat. Short crust pastry can be made by using: *a* all lard; *b* half lard and half margarine; *c* all white cooking fat. All lard makes a very rich pastry which is lovely to eat but difficult to handle; half lard and half margarine makes a slightly harder pastry which is much easier to handle; all white cooking fat makes a good pastry which is easy to roll out. Which fat would *you* use for short crust pastry? Can you remember the proportion of fat to flour?

Short crust pastry is made by the **rubbing-in** method. The fat is lightly rubbed into the flour until the mixture looks like fine breadcrumbs. Cold water is then added (5 ml for 25 g flour) and a stiff, dry paste is formed. The paste is rolled out lightly on a floured board and after being shaped, it is baked in a hot oven.

If white cooking fat is being used, a little flour is put into a bowl, the fat is added and whisked well, and then the remaining flour is stirred into the mixture.

2 Suet pastry

Suet pastry can be used for savoury and sweet dishes, which are to be steamed or baked. Steaming is the best method for cooking suet pastry because the long, moist cooking makes the pastry light and digestible. Baking tends to harden suet pastry.

The fat used in suet pastry is suet. Instead of being rubbed into the flour the fat is cut into small pieces or shreds, and stirred in. Water is then added until the mixture forms a soft, elastic dough. The pastry should be cooked and then served immediately. Suet pastry will go hard if it is allowed to stand.

3 Flaky pastry

This is one of the richer pastries and because more than half fat to flour is used the rubbing-in method is unsuitable. The fats used can be: *a* all lard; *b* half lard and half margarine; *c* all white cooking fat.

The fat is placed on a plate and softened with a fork until it is creamy. It is then divided into four quarters and one quarter is rubbed into the flour. Water is added to this

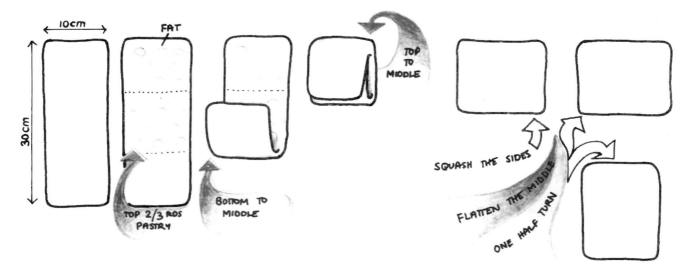

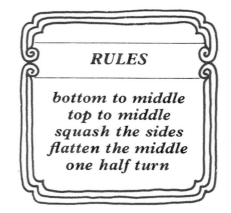

mixture to form an elastic paste, which is then rolled out to a long, thin strip (about 30 cm by 10 cm).

The sides must always be kept straight and the corners square. The oblong is then marked into thirds and a second quarter of the fat is put on the top two-thirds of the pastry.

The fat is added in small blobs which are put in straight lines. The pastry is then folded. Say the rules to yourself as you fold the pastry.

This is repeated until the remaining two quarters of fat have been added.

Flaky pastry should be put into a cool place for at least $\frac{1}{2}$ hour before it is used. It can be used for sweet or savoury dishes which are then baked in a hot oven.

RULES

bottom to middle
top to middle
squash the sides
flatten the middle
one half turn

4 Rough puff pastry

This is another of the richer pastries. The fat used can be: *a* all lard; *b* half lard and half margarine; *c* all white cooking fat. The fat is cut into walnut-sized pieces and stirred into the flour. Cold water is then added and the lumpy paste is kneaded together. Rough puff pastry is rolled out in exactly the same way as flaky pastry. After three rollings the pastry is left to cool before being used for savoury or sweet dishes. Rough puff pastry is baked in a hot oven.

There are several other kinds of pastries which we have not mentioned at all. Amongst these are *choux, flan, puff, hot water crust* pastries. These are not used very often. Their main uses are:

choux pastry	éclairs, savoury puff balls
flan pastry	fruit flans
puff pastry	patties, vol-au-vent cases
hot water crust pastry	pork pies, veal and ham pies, sausage and egg pies

Pastry and flan fillings

Here are some suggested fillings that you might like to try when making pies, tarts and pasties:

Savoury: cheese and onion; minced beef and onion; cooked chicken; sausagemeat; cooked ham and sliced tomato; mixed vegetables.

Sweet: apple; blackberry and apple; plum; gooseberry; blackcurrant; mincemeat; lemon curd; treacle.

Here are some suggested fillings for flans:

Savoury: bacon and egg; chicken and mushroom in white sauce; flaked cod in white sauce.

Sweet: lemon meringue; egg custard; fruit salad; fresh fruit in jelly or arrowroot glaze.

Using frozen pastry

Frozen pastry is an excellent substitute for home-made pastry. It is more expensive to use but always gives good results. Frozen puff pastries are often so light that they rise and rise in the oven and unless you are careful, pastry lids can pop off and pie lids can lift up. However, for the busy cook frozen pastries are invaluable.

When using frozen pastries it is important to remember:

1 to let the pastry thaw before trying to roll it;
2 to roll the pastry *very* thinly;
3 to seal all edges well together;
4 to bake in a very hot oven.

Think and Do

1. Collect as many pictures of pastry dishes as you can find in magazines. Stick them neatly into your books and underneath each one print the name of the type of pastry that has been used.

2. Copy the following sentences into your books, and write in the missing words:

a. The raising agent in suet pastry is ....

b. The proportion of fat to flour for flaky pastry is ....

c. If all lard is used when making short crust pastry, a rich, ... pastry is formed.

d. A .... oven is used for baking short crust pastry.

e. .... water should be used in pastry-making.

f. .... is the raising agent in rough puff pastry.

g. Frozen pastry should be .... before being used.

h. .... makes suet pastry light and digestible.

3. Suggest four savoury dishes and four sweet dishes that can be made with short crust pastry.

4. The following are famous pastry dishes. Look at a map of the British Isles and see where each of the place names is.
Melton Mowbray pie; Denby Dale pie; Cornish pasties; Dorset apple dumplings; Eccles cakes; Bakewell tart; Banbury puffs; Chorley cakes; Coventry god cakes; Hawkshead cakes; Shropshire fidget cake; Richmond Maids of Honour.

5. Which is the odd one out in each of the following groups? Why?

a. Eccles cakes; Bakewell tart; treacle tart; Banbury puffs.

b. Jam layer pudding; steak and kidney pudding; minced meat dumpling; lemon curd tart.

c. Blackberry tartlet; jam puff; vanilla slice; cream horn.

6. Which pastry would you use for each of the following dishes?
Sausage rolls; mince tarts; jam roly-poly; vanilla slices; chicken vol-au-vent; éclairs; dumplings; pork pie; Bakewell tart; lemon meringue pie.

7. Solve the following crossword.

Clues across

1. Jam roly-poly can be cooked this way
2. The proportion of fat to flour in short crust pastry
3. A fat used in making flaky pastry
4. A concentrated source of energy used in pastry-making

Clues down

1. Used in pastry-making to add flavour
5. Pastry used for dumplings
6. The consistency of rough puff pastry

8. Copy the following paragraph into your books. For each blank space choose the correct word from the list of words at the bottom.

'Short crust pastry can be used for .... and .... dishes. ...., ... and white cooking fat are the three fats that can be used. The proportion of fat to flour is .... The fat is .... into the flour with the .... until the mixture looks like fine .... water is added until a .... dough is formed. Short crust pastry should be rolled out on a lightly .... board and after shaping, baked in a .... oven.'

Breadcrumbs; hot; cold; fingertips; sweet; lard; stiff; savoury; margarine; half; floured; rubbed.

9. Suggest a pastry dish suitable for each of the following:
a. a vegetarian's lunch; *b.* a picnic meal; *c.* a New Year's Eve buffet party; *d.* a traditional North of England dish; *e.* a garden party; *f.* refreshments at a Parents-Teachers evening; *g.* a hot meal after a hockey match; *h.* a pastry dish using milk.

10. Look back to page 126 and copy the drawing into your notebook of how fat is added in flaky pastry.

11. Make two batches of sausage rolls. Use frozen puff pastry for the first batch, and your own pastry for the second. After the sausage rolls have been baked, compare the results. Work out the cost of each batch.

Chapter 18
Cake-making

In this chapter we are going to learn about the different methods of making cakes and how some of the common faults in cake-making can be avoided.

Food value of cakes
Cakes are mainly *carbohydrate.* They contain large amounts of *starch* (in the form of flour), and *sugar. Protein* and *vitamins* are present in cakes which have been made with eggs. Most cakes also contain large amounts of *fat.*

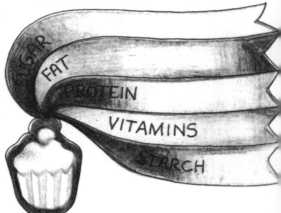

CAKES ARE ENERGY-GIVING FOODS

Figures beware! A word of warning
Because cakes are rich in carbohydrate they are fattening foods and should only be eaten in small amounts. The worst offenders are the cakes which ooze with cream or butter icing. They may be delicious to eat but keep one eye on the waistline.

There are four main methods of making cakes:
1 the rubbing-in method;
2 the creaming method;
3 the whisking method;
4 the melting method.

1 The rubbing-in method
This method is used for making *plain* cakes. Cakes made by the rubbing-in method are called 'plain' because they do not contain a large amount of fat. The usual amount of fat to add

is half the weight of the flour being used. For example, for 100 g flour use 50 g fat and for 200 g flour use 100 g fat. *Less* than half fat to flour can be used but not *more* than half fat to flour.

In this method the fat is rubbed into the flour with the *tips of the fingers,* until the mixture resembles fine bread-crumbs. Do not use the palms of your hands when rubbing in because these are the warmest parts of your hands and the heat will make the mixture sticky and difficult to manage. Using your fingertips will help to keep the mixture cool (see drawing on p. 118).

All the dry ingredients are added to the mixture before the liquids. The raising agent in plain cakes is *baking powder.* This gives off the gas called carbon dioxide, which makes the cakes rise.

A rubbed-in cake mixture can be turned into a variety of dishes. It may be steamed as a pudding or baked as a large fruit cake. It may have any of the following flavourings added: cherries, coconut, cocoa, chopped nuts, orange peel, carraway seeds, mixed spice, ginger. Can you think of any other flavourings which you could add if you wanted to make a large cake? Rubbed-in mixtures can also be used for small cakes which may be baked in pattie tins or flat on a baking sheet. Raspberry buns, rock buns, and scones are examples of a rubbed-in mixture which is baked as small buns.

The consistency of the mixture is important for a good result. Here is a guide to help you:

Dish	Consistency
Large, rubbed-in cake e.g. coconut loaf	Soft consistency (just dropping from a spoon)
Small, rubbed-in buns e.g. raspberry buns	Stiff, dry mixture (should be able to hold a fork upright)

Large plain cakes are baked in a moderate oven, but small plain cakes are baked in a hot oven.

Dish	Type of oven	Gas	Electric
Large rubbed-in plain cake	moderate	5	*190°C*
Small rubbed-in buns	hot	7	*220°C*

Points to remember when making rubbed-in mixtures

1 Any tins which are to be used must be prepared before you begin. For small cakes, grease or flour the baking sheet, and for large cakes, grease the cake tin well.

2 Sieve flour, salt and baking powder together. This will trap air into the mixture to make it lighter; it will mix the ingredients together thoroughly and it will crumble any lumps that are present.

3 Rub the fat in lightly. At all times keep the mixture as cool as possible.

4 Add any remaining dry ingredients before you add any liquid.

5 Check that you obtain the correct consistency, and that the cakes are baked at the correct heat.

Common faults in rubbed-in mixtures

Fault	Reason	How to avoid
a **Very dry cake**	Mixture not of a soft, dropping consistency before being baked	*Add enough liquid to give correct consistency*
b **Fruit which has sunk to bottom of cake**	Fruit has been too heavy *or* too much moisture has been added	*Clean fruit in flour* not *in water. Do not make mixture too wet*
c **Cake which has risen and cracked on top**	Baked in too hot an oven *or* too near the top of the oven	*Bake large plain cakes at gas mark 5 (190°C) and in the middle of the oven*
d **Small cakes which have lost shape and which have spread out on baking tin**	Too wet a mixture before baking *or* too cool an oven	*Do not add too much liquid. Small, plain cakes should be of a dry consistency. Bake at the top of a hot oven*

The diagram summarizes some of the important facts to re-member when making rubbed-in mixtures.

2 The creaming method

This method is used for making **rich** cakes. Cakes made by this method are called 'rich' because they contain large amounts of fat. The usual amount of fat to use is $\frac{2}{3}$ or $\frac{3}{4}$ the weight of the flour being used. In some creamed cakes the amount of fat actually equals the amount of flour. In this method the fat and sugar are mixed together using a wooden spoon or plastic scraper, until they become white in colour and fluffy and light in texture. This process is called **cream-ing** the fat and sugar. It is during this stage that air is beaten into the mixture and this helps to make the cake light. The eggs are then beaten into the mixture drop by drop. The flour and baking powder is then lightly **folded** into the mixture of fat, sugar and eggs. Do not stir the mixture too much at this stage or some air may be beaten out of the mixture. Always fold in the flour gently using a metal spoon.

The raising agents in rich cakes are **baking powder** and **air.** Baking powder is added to the mixture and air is in-cluded by:

a creaming the fat and sugar;
b beating in the eggs;
c sieving the flour and baking powder (before adding).

A creamed mixture can be turned into a variety of dishes. It can be steamed or baked as a pudding. It can be baked as a large cake, a sandwich cake, or as small buns.

All creamed mixtures should have a **soft** consistency. If a mixture looks too dry when it is finished add either some warm water, milk or more egg. Large creamed cakes are baked in a warm oven, but sandwich cakes and small buns are baked in a slightly hotter oven.

Dish	Type of oven	Gas	Electric
Large creamed cake	warm	*3*	*170°C*
Sandwich cake	warm	*4*	*180°C*
Small creamed buns	moderate	*5*	*190°C*

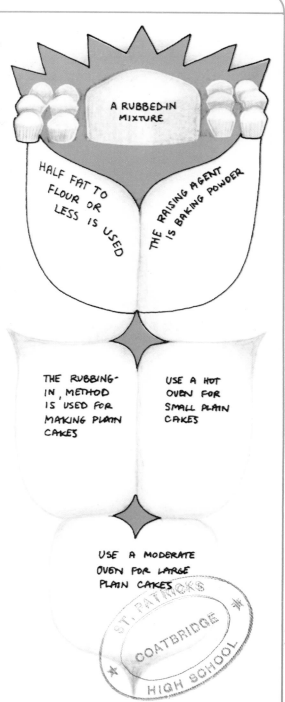

A RUBBED-IN MIXTURE

HALF FAT TO FLOUR OR LESS IS USED

THE RAISING AGENT IS BAKING POWDER

THE RUBBING-IN METHOD IS USED FOR MAKING PLAIN CAKES

USE A HOT OVEN FOR SMALL PLAIN CAKES

USE A MODERATE OVEN FOR LARGE PLAIN CAKES

Points to remember when making creamed mixtures

1 Prepare the cake tins. For small cakes either use pattie tins which have been greased or paper bun cases. Large cake tins should be greased and lined with greaseproof paper. Have all the ingredients at room temperature.

2 Always cream the fat and sugar well before you add the eggs. Many people believe that it is this stage that decides the success of a cake. Remember that you can never over-cream so be patient and cream the mixture well.

3 Lightly beat the eggs before you add them to the creamed fat and sugar. Add the eggs a drop at a time and beat well between each addition. If the mixture looks lumpy and 'curdled', stir in a little flour before adding more egg.

4 The flour and baking powder should be sieved well before adding to the cake mixture. Fold the flour in very lightly and then add any flavouring, e.g. currants, coconut, sultanas, chocolate drops, cherries.

5 Check that the mixture is of a soft consistency before being baked.

A CREAMED CAKE MIXTURE BY THE ALTERNATIVE ALL-IN-ONE METHOD

USE APPROX THE SAME AMOUNT OF SR FLOUR AS FAT AND ADD EXTRA BAKING POWDER

MIX DRY INGREDIENTS IN BOWL THEN DROP IN REST AND BEAT

USE SOFT MARGARINE

Common faults in a creamed cake

Fault	Reason	How to avoid
a Cake which has sunk in middle	Mixture not cooked enough *or* moved too suddenly before properly cooked	*Do not allow draughts to get in the oven during cooking. Test with a warmed skewer before removing cake from oven*
b Cake which has risen and cracked in middle	Baked in too hot an oven *or* too near the top of the oven. Too much baking powder may have been used	*Bake at the correct heat for the size of the cake. Measure baking powder accurately*
c Cake which has crisp, speckled surface	Sugar has not been creamed sufficiently *or* mixture not scraped from the sides of the mixing bowl enough	*Cream fat and sugar together well. Keep scraping the mixture from the sides of the bowl during mixing*

The diagram summarizes some important facts to remember when making a creamed cake mixture.

3 The whisking method

This method is used for making **sponge** cakes. A true sponge cake does not have any fat in the mixture and for this reason it will not keep for a long time. After a few days it becomes dry. Sponges are delicious eaten when fresh because they are very fluffy and light. There are only three ingredients in a whisked sponge mixture: eggs, sugar and flour. Equal weights of sugar and flour are used. The weight of egg should be double the weight of sugar (e.g. 2 eggs for 50 g sugar).

In this method the eggs and sugar are whisked together until they turn thick and creamy. An electric mixer, a rotary whisk or a hand whisk may be used. During this process, air is trapped into the mixture and it is this that makes the sponge light. The flour, after being sieved, is then carefully folded into the mixture with a metal spoon. Always fold in the flour **gently** with a cutting movement.

The raising agent in a true sponge is **air** and no chemical raising agent should be needed. Some people, however, prefer to add a little baking powder to the flour as a safeguard to ensure a really light sponge.

Whisked mixtures are baked in a hot oven.

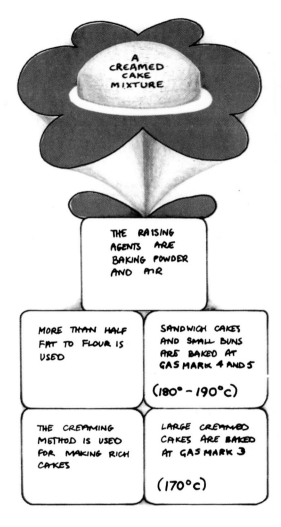

A CREAMED CAKE MIXTURE

THE RAISING AGENTS ARE BAKING POWDER AND AIR

MORE THAN HALF FAT TO FLOUR IS USED

SANDWICH CAKES AND SMALL BUNS ARE BAKED AT GAS MARK 4 AND 5 (180° – 190°C)

THE CREAMING METHOD IS USED FOR MAKING RICH CAKES

LARGE CREAMED CAKES ARE BAKED AT GAS MARK 3 (170°C)

Dish	Type of oven	Gas	Electric
Whisked mixture	very hot	8	230°C

Points to remember when making whisked mixtures

1 Prepare the cake tins.

2 Always whisk the eggs and sugar together until creamy and fluffy. The mixture should then be stiff enough to leave a trail when dropped from the end of the whisk. If you are using a hand whisk it is quicker to whisk the eggs and sugar together over a bowl or pan of hot water, but be careful.

3 Carefully fold in the sieved flour using a metal spoon. Remember that if you stir the mixture harshly you will lose some of the air which you are relying on to make your cake light.

4 A whisked mixture should look thick and fluffy before being baked. If you are making a Swiss roll, where the mixture has to be spread over a large area, it helps to add two tablespoonfuls of boiling water.

Common faults in a whisked cake

Fault	Reason	How to avoid
a **Sponge which is dry**	Not fresh enough	*Do not try to store sponges. Eat them when they are fresh*
b **Dry, powdery patches in cake**	Flour not folded in sufficiently	*Fold in carefully until there is no flour showing*
c **Swiss roll that cracks when rolled**	Baked for too long	*Time the cooking exactly*

The diagram summarizes some important facts to remember when making a whisked mixture.

4 The melting method

This method is not used often in cookery. The dishes that can be made by it are very few, the best known being parkin and gingerbread.

In this method all the dry ingredients are placed in a mixing bowl, while the syrup, sugar and fat are melted in a saucepan. The melted ingredients are then poured into the mixing bowl and everything is mixed together.

The raising agent is **bicarbonate of soda,** which gives off carbon dioxide to make the mixture rise. Melted mixtures usually contain a large amount of sugar, so in order to prevent burning cook in a warm oven.

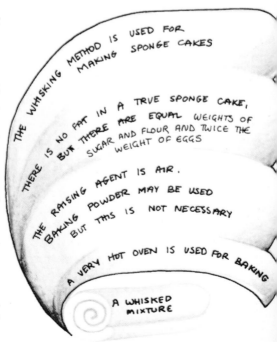

THE WHISKING METHOD IS USED FOR MAKING SPONGE CAKES

THERE IS NO FAT IN A TRUE SPONGE CAKE, BUT THERE ARE EQUAL WEIGHTS OF SUGAR AND FLOUR AND TWICE THE WEIGHT OF EGGS

THE RAISING AGENT IS AIR. BAKING POWDER MAY BE USED BUT THIS IS NOT NECESSARY

A VERY HOT OVEN IS USED FOR BAKING

A WHISKED MIXTURE

Dish	Type of oven	Gas	Electric
Melted mixtures	warm	*3 or 4*	*170°–180°C*

Points to remember when making melted mixtures

1 Prepare the cake tins.

2 Always weigh the ingredients accurately. Too much syrup or treacle will spoil the texture.

3 When melting the syrup, fat and sugar, always use a **low** heat. The ingredients must not be allowed to sizzle and become too hot.

4 The completed mixture should be of a wet, dropping consistency similar to that of a batter.

Common faults in a melted mixture

Fault	Reason	*How to avoid*
a **Cake that has cracks on top and a dry texture**	Baked in too hot an oven	*Bake at gas mark 3 or 4 (170°—180°C)*
b **Cake that has sunk in middle**	Either not cooked sufficiently *or* too heavy with treacle or syrup	*Cake should feel firm when brought out of oven. Weigh the ingredients accurately*

NOTE. It is interesting to note that in the North of England it is considered a good sign if a parkin sinks in the middle. This means that the cake is sticky and rich in syrup or treacle.

Some simple cake decorations

When serving small buns add a simple decoration to make them look more attractive. Neatly cover them with *water icing* (icing sugar mixed with water) and top them with glacé cherries, chopped nuts, or chocolate drops. Can you think of any other colourful decorations which are suitable for small buns?

Sandwich cakes may be decorated with *feather icing* (water icing used in two contrasting colours to give a feathery effect).

Butter icing is also suitable for sandwich cakes. (Butter icing is icing made by sieving icing sugar with creamed butter.) Butter icing can be spread over a sandwich cake and patterned using a fork or knife.

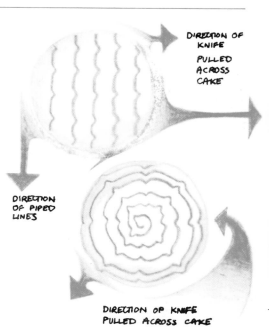

DIRECTION OF KNIFE PULLED ACROSS CAKE

DIRECTION OF PIPED LINES

DIRECTION OF KNIFE PULLED ACROSS CAKE

This type of icing can also be piped on to a cake using an icing bag and nozzle.

Another simple, but very effective, way of decorating a cake is to place sweets on the top immediately it has come out of the oven. The heat of the cake slightly melts the sweets and an attractive pattern can be produced. Peppermint creams and marshmallows are particularly effective.

Royal icing (icing sugar mixed with egg white) is used to decorate special occasion cakes such as wedding, Christmas and birthday cakes. Royal icing can be piped on to cakes or it may be spread roughly over a surface to give a 'snowy' effect. This is an ideal way of decorating Christmas cakes.

A quick way of decorating a large cake is to cover the cake with a fancy d'oyley and then lightly sprinkle the cake with icing sugar. The d'oyley must then be carefully lifted from the cake, and a delicate pattern of icing sugar will be left.

Try to experiment yourself and see how many different ways you can think of for decorating cakes. Remember to keep your patterns **simple.** They are always more effective.

Using bought cake mixes

Packet cake mixes which can be bought at your local grocer's shop are very simple to use. Clear instructions for making the cake are given on the sides of the packet and if these are followed carefully very good cakes can be made in only a few minutes. It is useful to have a packet cake mix in the larder in case of unexpected guests.

Cake mixes are a great saver of time and energy. A lot of time can be saved by not having to weigh ingredients and prepare the mixture yourself. All that is needed is the addition of a liquid (usually an egg) and the mixture is ready to be baked.

When trying a cake mix remember to:

1 Read the instructions carefully.
2 Check the amount of liquid to be added.
3 Bake at the oven heat stated.

Packet cakes are best if they are eaten fresh because occasionally the flavour of the chemical raising agent becomes pronounced after a few days. Which cake mixes have you tried and liked?

icing being piped onto cake

Think and Do

1 Look in magazines and try to find a picture of some cakes. Stick it into your book and copy the diagram like this:

Plain cakes are made by the rubbing-in method

Rich cakes are made by the creaming method

Stick your picture here

Gingerbreads, parkins are made by the melting method

Sponge cakes are made by the whisking method

2. List as many different cakes as you can think of that can be made from a rubbed-in mixture.

3. Describe in your own words how you would:

a. clean dried fruit ready for a Christmas cake;

b. line a Swiss roll tin;

c. rub fat into flour.

4. Which method would you use when making each of the following cakes?

a. Victoria sandwich   *f.* scones

b. parkin   *g.* raspberry buns

c. Swiss roll   *h.* Welsh cheesecakes

d. gingerbread   *i.* sponge drops

e. rock buns   *j.* flapjacks

5. How many flavours can you think of which can be added to a creamed cake mixture?

6. Choose one word from the words in the brackets to complete each of the following sentences. Write the completed sentences into your books.

a. When making a creamed mixture the two ingredients that must first be mixed together are fat and (egg, sugar, baking powder).

b. The raising agent in a melted mixture is (self-raising flour, air, bicarbonate of soda).

c. Large rich cakes should be baked in a (hot, medium, cool) oven.

d. The proportion of fat to flour in a rubbed-in mixture should not be more than ($\frac{3}{4}$, $\frac{1}{2}$, $\frac{2}{3}$).

e. There is no (sugar, egg, fat) in a whisked mixture.

f. If a creamed mixture begins to curdle when you add the (egg, milk, fat) stir in a little flour.

g. Cakes made by the rubbing-in method are called (simnel, dry, plain) cakes.

h. (Carbon dioxide, Hydrogen, Nitrous oxide) is the gas given off when baking powder is put into cakes.

7. Design a poster to make people more aware of the dangers of eating too many cakes.

8. The following ingredients are often used in cake-making:

a. sultanas; *b.* syrup; *c.* self-raising flour; *d.* demerara sugar; *e.* carraway seeds; *f.* candied peel; *g.* mixed spice; *h.* coconut; *i.* cocoa; *j.* raisins.

Visit your local grocer and find out their present prices.

9. Name the raising agent in each of the following cakes:

a. scones; *b.* sponge fingers; *c.* raspberry buns; *d.* orange sandwich cake; *e.* parkin; *f.* Swiss roll; *g.* meringues; *h.* madeleines.

10. Make two sandwich cakes. Prepare one of the mixtures yourself and use a packet mix for the other. After the cakes have been baked, compare the two results and record in your books their:

a. appearance; *b.* cost; *c.* taste.

Part Four

Recipes

Here are some recipes which you might like to try for yourself. Choose a suitable dish for the meal you have in mind and before you begin:

1 Read through the recipe carefully, and make sure that you understand it. Remember that Chapter 15 is all about Understanding Recipes, and you may wish to turn to it for revision.

2 Check that you have *the correct ingredients and equipment* and *enough time* in which to make and bake the dish.

How to use this recipe section

The recipes are divided into groups. There are some suggested dishes for each main meal of the day. At the end of each recipe there is a menu, showing how the dish can become part of a balanced meal. As you prepare each dish, plan in your mind which accompanying dishes *you* would like to turn your dish into a complete meal. Try to work out which part of the meal must be prepared first and then which dish you would make next, so that the complete meal can be ready at the same time.

Choosing dishes in which to bake and serve

If a recipe requires an *ovenproof* dish, this means that the dish must be able to stand the heat inside an oven. It must not melt or crack when heated. Ovenproof dishes can be made of: thick glass, thick earthenware or pottery, enamel, stainless steel or aluminium. Do you think that polythene and china dishes would be suitable dishes in which to bake?

If a recipe requires a *casserole* dish, this means that the dish must have a lid. When a casserole dish is not available an ordinary ovenproof dish can be used with a temporary lid using: a heavy glass or tin plate, greaseproof paper or aluminium foil.

The *size* of dish used is also important. Always use a dish that is too big rather than too small. Each recipe states the type and size needed. A 10 decilitre dish means one that will hold 10 decilitres of liquid. If you are not sure that the dish you want to use is big enough, fill a litre measure with water. Pour the water into the dish and see if the dish will easily

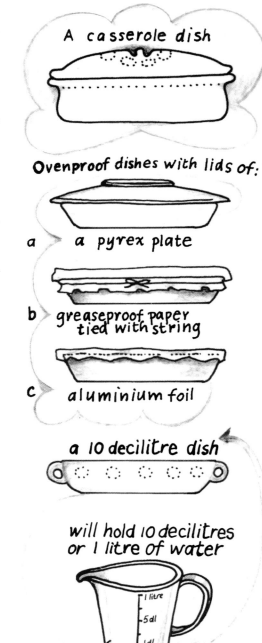

A casserole dish

Ovenproof dishes with lids of:

a ▷ a pyrex plate

b ▷ greaseproof paper tied with string

c ▷ aluminium foil

a 10 decilitre dish

will hold 10 decilitres or 1 litre of water

hold 10 decilitres. Dishes can be round, oval, oblong or square. The shape is not important, but the size is.

Try to serve your dishes attractively. A splash of colour from a garnish will brighten the plainest of dishes.

When you have made each of the dishes in this recipe section, you will be ready to cook more adventuresome meals. Use the recipe books in your school library and collect as many different ideas as you can for the main meals of the day.

List of Recipes

BREAKFAST DISHES

1 *Fresh Grapefruit*
2 *Scrambled Egg*
3 *Welsh Rarebit*
4 *Fried Bacon and Egg*
5 *Boiled Egg*

SAVOURY DISHES
for Dinner or Lunch

6 *Hotpot*
7 *Stuffed Breast of Lamb*
8 *Steak Casserole*
9 *Fish Pie*
10 *Cheese and Potato Pie*

VEGETABLES
for Dinner or Lunch

11 *Boiled Potatoes*
12 *Chipped Potatoes*
13 *Grilled Tomatoes*
14 *Boiled 'Frozen' Vegetables*
15 *Boiled 'Fresh' Green Vegetables*

SAUCES
for Dinner or Lunch

16 **Gravy**
17 **White Sauce**
18 **Mint Sauce**
Custard Sauce (see recipe 29)

HOT PUDDINGS
for Dinner or Lunch

19 **Rice Pudding**
20 **Bread and Butter Pudding**
21 **Apple Crumble**
22 **Steamed Jam Sponge**
23 **Fruit Pie**

SAVOURY DISHES
for High Tea or Supper

24 **Egg Salad**
25 **Stuffed Cheese Potatoes**
26 **Cornish Pasties**
27 **Sausage Rolls**
28 **Egg Mayonnaise**

COLD SWEETS
for High Tea or Supper

29 **Banana Custard**
30 **Trifle**
31 **Blancmange**
32 **Fruit Salad**
33 **Fruit in Jelly**

CAKES AND BISCUITS
for Afternoon Tea
and High Tea

34 **Shortbread Biscuits**
35 **Rock Buns**
36 **Oatmeal Scones**
37 **Victoria Sandwich**
38 **Flapjacks or Firelighters**

Fresh Grapefruit

Serves 2

Ingredients needed
1 grapefruit
4 × 5 ml spoons sugar

Equipment needed
1 vegetable knife
1 chopping board
a 5 ml spoon

Serving dish needed
2 small fruit dishes

Preparations
1 Collect the equipment.
2 Wash your hands.
3 Collect the ingredients.

Method
1 Cut the grapefruit in half, around the 'equator'.
2 Using a sharp knife, cut the flesh of the fruit from the pith (the white part of the skin).
3 Separate each of the segments.
4 Sprinkle 2 × 5 ml spoons sugar over each half of grapefruit.
5 Put each grapefruit half in an individual dish and decorate with a cherry or a drop of red jam.

Menu

Breakfast

— ❋ —

Grapefruit

Fried bacon,
mushroom and tomato
Bread and Butter

Coffee

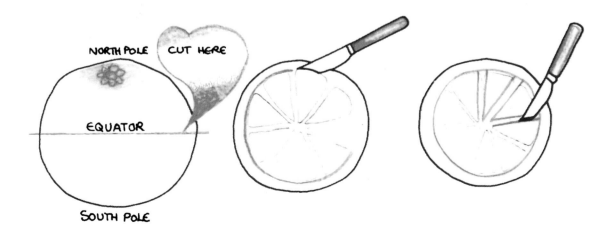

Scrambled Egg

Serves 4

Ingredients needed
6 large eggs
25 g margarine or butter
40 ml milk
¼ × 5 ml spoon salt
sprinkle of pepper

Flavourings
4 × 20 ml spoons chopped
   cooked bacon
4 chopped tomatoes
100 g grated cheese
1 × 5 ml spoon chopped
   fresh herbs

Equipment
1 small saucepan
1 wooden spoon
1 cup
a 20 ml spoon
a 5 ml spoon

Serving dish
1 large round,
   or oval plate
or 4 dinner plates

Preparations
1 Collect the equipment.
2 Wash your hands.
3 Collect the ingredients.
4 Put the serving dishes in a warm place.
5 If a flavoured, scrambled egg is being made, prepare the flavouring (i.e. cheese should be grated; tomatoes should be washed and chopped into tiny pieces; fresh herbs washed and then chopped finely).

Method
1 Over a low heat, gently melt the fat in the saucepan.
2 When the fat has melted, remove the pan from the heat, and add 40 ml milk.
3 Break each egg in turn into a cup to check that it is fresh and add to the saucepan.
4 Season with salt and pepper.
5 Most flavourings can be added before the mixture is cooked (but remember that cheese hardens when overcooked and therefore should be added **after** the mixture has been cooked).
6 Cook the mixture over a low heat, stirring all the time with a wooden spoon.
7 Cook until the mixture has thickened. Scrambled egg should be soft and creamy. If overcooked it turns dry and leathery, so do not cook for too long, once the mixture has thickened.

Breakfast
— ❋ —
Fruit juice
Cheese-flavoured
scrambled egg
with grilled tomatoes
Toast and marmalade
Tea

8 Either scrape the scrambled egg onto a large plate or divide it amongst individual plates. A garnish of parsley adds colour and interest.

9 Scrambled egg can be served in several ways as a breakfast dish. Here are some ideas:
Scrambled egg on toast
Flavoured scrambled egg with bread fingers
Scrambled egg with grilled kidneys
Scrambled egg with fried bacon and bread
Cooked tomato (or potato) cases stuffed with scrambled egg.

Welsh Rarebit

Serves 4

Ingredients
4 slices bread
50 g butter
150 g cheese
40 ml milk
salt and pepper
1 tomato
sprig of parsley

Equipment
1 grill pan
1 basin
1 round-bladed knife
1 grater
a 20 ml spoon

Serving dish
4 plates

Preparations
1 Collect the equipment.
2 Heat the grill.
3 Wash your hands.
4 Weigh the ingredients.
5 Grate the cheese into a basin.

Method
1 Place the bread on the grill pan and toast until a golden brown colour on both sides.
2 Add 40 ml milk and a dash of salt and pepper to the grated cheese. Stir well.
3 Lightly butter the toast and spread the cheese paste mixture on the top of each slice.
4 Decorate each Welsh rarebit with a slice of tomato.
5 Replace the Welsh rarebits under the hot grill and cook until the cheese has melted and turned a golden brown in colour.
6 Garnish with sprigs of parsley and serve while hot on individual plates.

Menu

Breakfast

— ✳ —

Cornflakes
Welsh rarebit
Glass of milk
An apple

Fried Bacon and Egg

Serves 4

Ingredients needed
4 rashers bacon
4 eggs
25 g lard

Equipment needed
1 frying pan
1 fork
1 fish slice
1 pair kitchen scissors
1 cup
a 20 ml spoon

Serving dish needed
1 oval, or round, large plate
or 4 dinner plates

Preparations
1 Collect the equipment.
2 Wash your hands.
3 Collect the ingredients.
4 Using a pair of kitchen scissors, cut the rind from the rashers of bacon.
Snip with diagonal, half-inch cuts down the length of each rasher. Cut each rasher into three pieces.
5 Put the serving dishes in a warm place.

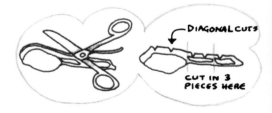

DIAGONAL CUTS

CUT IN 3 PIECES HERE

Method
1 Over a low heat, gently melt the fat in the frying pan.
2 When a faint, blue haze begins to rise from the fat, place the rashers of bacon in the pan. Fry for 2 minutes.
3 Using a fork, turn each rasher of bacon and cook for a further 2 minutes on the other side.
4 Remove the bacon when cooked, and place it on a warm plate.
5 Turn the heat under the frying pan lower.
6 Break each egg in turn into a cup to check that it is fresh, and then carefully pour the egg into the hot fat. In a large frying pan 4 eggs can be cooked at the same time.
7 With a spoon, baste the yolk of the eggs in hot fat. Fry for 2 minutes.
8 Using a fish slice, carefully remove the eggs and slide them on to a warm plate.

Menu

Breakfast

— ❋ —

Porridge
Fried bacon and eggs
Bread

Coffee

Boiled Egg

Serves 4

Ingredients needed
4 large eggs

Equipment needed
1 small saucepan
a 20 ml spoon

Serving dish needed
4 egg cups
4 small plates

Preparations
1 Collect the equipment.
2 Wash your hands.
3 Half fill the saucepan with cold water and place the saucepan over a low heat.

Method
1 When the water begins to simmer (i.e. tiny bubbles rise to the surface) gently lower each egg into the saucepan on a tablespoon. Notice the **time.**
2 Keep the water in the saucepan gently simmering and **not** boiling.
3 For an egg that has a 'runny' yolk, simmer for 4 minutes. For an egg that has a slightly firmer yolk, simmer for 5 minutes. For a hard-boiled egg that will be sliced when making salads, simmer for 10 minutes.
4 When cooked, lift the eggs out of the saucepan and place them in the egg cups. Stand the egg cups on small plates.
5 Boiled eggs are served hot with fingers of bread and butter or toast.

Menu

Breakfast

— ❋ —

Stewed prunes

Boiled egg
Bread and butter fingers

Toast and marmalade
Tea

Hotpot

Serves 4

Ingredients needed

1 kg potatoes
1 large onion
300 g stewing steak

1 × 5 ml spoon salt
sprinkle of pepper
375 ml water or stock

Equipment needed

1 vegetable knife
1 plate
1 chopping board

1 pair kitchen scissors
1 measure
a 5 ml spoon

Serving dish needed

a 10 dl ovenproof dish with lid or a 10 dl casserole dish

Preparations

1 Collect the equipment.
2 Turn on the oven at gas mark 5 or 190°C.
3 Grease the ovenproof dish.
4 Wash your hands.
5 Weigh the ingredients.
6 Wipe the meat and cut it into 1·5 cm cubes using kitchen scissors. Remove any large pieces of fat.
7 Peel the onion and slice it into rings.
8 Peel and wash the potatoes. Cut them evenly into slices about 1 cm thick.

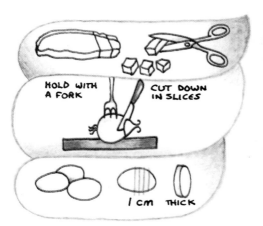

HOLD WITH A FORK   CUT DOWN IN SLICES

1 CM   THICK

Method

1 Place half of the meat in the bottom of the greased oven-proof dish.
2 Add half of the sliced onion and cover with half of the sliced potatoes.
3 Place the rest of the meat, onion and potatoes in layers, finishing with a layer of potatoes.
4 Add 1 × 5 ml spoon salt and a sprinkle of pepper and pour the 375 ml water or stock into the dish.
5 Cover the dish with a piece of aluminium foil. If a casserole dish is being used, place the lid on the dish before cooking.
6 Bake in the middle of the oven for 1½ hours.
7 Remove the lid.
8 Cook for a further ½ hour. This will brown and crisp the top layer of potatoes.
9 This dish can be served with pickled red cabbage for high tea and supper, or with a green vegetable for dinner and lunch.

Menu

Dinner

— ❋ —

Hotpot
Cabbage

Fresh fruit salad
Cream

Stuffed Breast of Lamb

Serves 4

Ingredients needed

I breast of lamb	*50 g breadcrumbs*
I onion	*25 g shredded suet*
2 carrots	*½ × 5 ml spoon dried*
I × 5 ml spoon salt	*herbs*
sprinkle of pepper	*½ beaten egg*
375 ml water or *stock*	*¼ × 5 ml spoon salt*

Equipment needed

I vegetable knife *I small basin*
I round-bladed knife *I measure*
I mixing bowl
I grater
I fork
a 20 ml spoon
a 5 ml spoon

Serving dish

a 10 dl casserole dish

Preparations

1 Collect the equipment.
2 Turn on the oven at gas mark 5 or 190°C.
3 Wash your hands.
4 Collect and weigh the ingredients.
5 With a sharp knife cut the bones from the breast of lamb. **Be careful.**
6 Peel and slice the onion and carrots.
7 Rub the bread into fine breadcrumbs using the grater.

Method

1 Place the breadcrumbs, shredded suet and dried herbs in a mixing bowl.
2 Add ¼ × 5 ml spoon salt.
3 Break the egg into a small basin and beat it lightly with a fork.
4 Add half the beaten egg to the dry ingredients in the mixing bowl. Stir well.
5 Spread the moist stuffing over the inside of the breast of lamb.
6 Roll the breast up tightly and fasten it with string or cotton.
7 Place the rolled breast in the casserole dish and add the vegetables.
8 Pour 375 ml water or stock into the dish and add 1 × 5 ml spoon salt and a dash of pepper. Place the lid on the casserole.
9 Cook in the middle of the oven for 2 hours.
10 Serve this dish with potatoes and a green vegetable.

Menu

Dinner
— ✳ —
Stuffed breast of lamb
New potatoes
Garden peas

Apricot shortcake
Cream

Steak Casserole

Serves 4

Ingredients needed
500 g stewing steak
1 large onion
200 g carrots
2 small parsnips
500 ml water or stock
1 × 5 ml spoon salt
sprinkle of pepper
50 g lard or dripping

Equipment needed
1 frying pan
1 fork
1 vegetable knife
1 plate
1 chopping board
1 measure
1 pair kitchen scissors
a 5 ml spoon

Serving dish needed
a 10 dl casserole dish

Preparations
1 Collect the equipment.
2 Turn on the oven at gas mark 5 or 190°C.
3 Wash your hands.
4 Collect the ingredients.
5 Peel and slice the onion.
6 Peel and slice the carrots and parsnips.
7 Cut the meat into 4 pieces, removing any large pieces of fat or gristle.

Method
1 Melt the lard or dripping in a frying pan.
2 When a blue haze begins to rise from the fat, fry the steak on both sides (2 minutes).
3 Using a fork, lift the browned steak from the frying pan and put it in the casserole dish.
4 Add the slices of onion, carrot and parsnips to the meat.
5 Add 1 × 5 ml spoon salt and a sprinkle of pepper.
6 Pour 500 ml water or stock over the ingredients.
7 Place the lid on the casserole dish or cover the dish with aluminium foil.
8 Bake in the middle of the oven for 2 hours.
9 This dish should be served with potatoes and a green vegetable.

Menu

Dinner

— ✳ —

Steak casserole
Jacket potatoes
Cabbage

Apple sponge
Custard

Fish Pie

Serves 4

Ingredients needed

500 g cod
1 kg potatoes
50 g margarine
40 ml milk
salt and pepper
1 lemon

2 tomatoes
sprig of parsley

Equipment needed

1 saucepan with lid
1 vegetable knife
1 chopping board
2 large plates
1 fork
1 potato masher
a 20 ml spoon

Serving dish needed

a 10 dl ovenproof dish

Preparations

1 Collect the equipment.
2 Grease the ovenproof dish.
3 Wash your hands.
4 Collect and weigh the ingredients.
5 Wipe the fish with a clean, damp cloth.
6 Peel and rinse the potatoes. Cut them into even-sized pieces.

Method

1 Place the potatoes in a large saucepan and add cold water and $\frac{1}{2} \times 5$ ml spoon salt.
2 Put the fish on a plate and sprinkle it with salt and pepper. Add a small knob (25 g) of margarine.
3 Cover the fish with another plate, and then put the two plates over the saucepan containing the potatoes.
4 Cook the potatoes for 20 minutes. (The steam from the boiling water will cook the fish.)
5 After 20 minutes, carefully remove the plates containing the fish. They will be ***hot.***
6 Test to see if the potatoes are cooked. If they are soft, when pierced with a knife, turn off the heat.
7 Strain all the liquid from the potatoes and mash them well with the potato masher. Add 25 g margarine and 40 ml milk to the saucepan. Beat in with a fork.
8 Remove any bones and skin from the fish using a knife and fork.

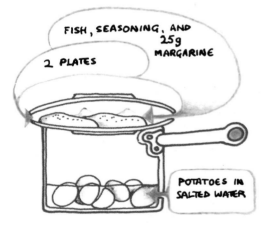

FISH, SEASONING, AND 25g MARGARINE

2 PLATES

POTATOES IN SALTED WATER

Menu

Dinner

— ❋ —

Fish pie
Brussels sprouts
Egg sauce

Lemon meringue pie

9 Flake the fish into tiny pieces.

10 Place the flaked fish and any liquid left on the plate, at the bottom of the ovenproof dish. Sprinkle it with chopped parsley.

11 Pile the creamed potatoes on the top. Level the top of the dish and decorate with slices of tomato and lemon.

12 Either brown the fish pie under a hot grill or bake it in a moderate oven (4, 180°C) for $\frac{1}{2}$ hour.

13 Serve this dish hot with a white sauce (see recipe 17) and a brightly-coloured vegetable.

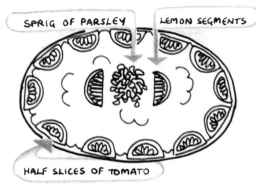

SPRIG OF PARSLEY   LEMON SEGMENTS

HALF SLICES OF TOMATO

10 *Cheese and Potato Pie* — Serves 4

Ingredients needed

1 kg potatoes
200 g hard cooking cheese
25 g margarine
40 ml milk
1 × 5 ml spoon salt
1 tomato
sprig of parsley

Equipment needed

1 large saucepan with lid
1 vegetable knife
1 plate
1 grater
1 potato masher
1 fork
a 20 ml spoon
a 5 ml spoon

Serving dish needed

1 large ovenproof dish

Preparations

1 Collect the equipment.
2 Wash your hands.
3 Weigh the ingredients.
4 Peel and wash the potatoes. Cut into even-sized pieces.
5 Grate the cheese.

Method

1 Cook the potatoes in salted water until they are soft (see recipe 11).

2 When soft, strain off the cooking liquid.

3 Mash the potatoes and add the margarine and milk. Beat well with a fork until the potatoes are soft and creamy.

4 Add $\frac{3}{4}$ of the grated cheese to the creamed potatoes and stir well.

5 Pile the cheese and potato mixture into an ovenproof dish.

6 Sprinkle the remaining cheese on the top.

7 Decorate the dish with slices of tomato.

8 Brown the pie under a hot grill.

9 Add a sprig of parsley and serve the dish while it is hot.

Menu

Dinner

— ❉ —

Cheese and potato pie
Grilled tomatoes
Onion sauce

Fruit flan
Cream

Boiled Potatoes

Serves 4

Ingredients needed
1 kg potatoes
½ × 5 ml spoon salt
25 g margarine
sprig of parsley

Equipment needed
1 chopping board
1 vegetable knife
or *potato peeler*
1 plate
1 mixing bowl
1 saucepan with a
*   tightly-fitting lid*
1 colander
a 5 ml spoon

Serving dish needed
a 10 dl casserole dish

Preparations
1 Collect the equipment.
2 Put the serving dish in a warm place.
3 Half fill a mixing bowl with cold water.
4 Wash your hands.
5 Using a vegetable knife or potato peeler, peel the potatoes thinly, letting the peelings fall onto a plate.
6 Put each peeled potato into the bowl of cold water. This stops the potatoes from turning brown.
7 When all the potatoes have been peeled, empty the bowl into the sink.
8 Rinse the bowl clean and refill it with fresh cold water.
9 Rinse each potato in turn under the cold water tap and return it to the bowl of water.
10 Chop a little parsley.

Method
1 Using a chopping board and vegetable knife, cut the clean potatoes into even-sized chunks (about the size of a medium tomato).
2 Put the cut potatoes into a saucepan.
3 Add cold water until the potatoes are almost covered.
4 Add ½ × 5 ml spoon salt and place the lid on the saucepan firmly.

A TOMATO

5 Put the saucepan over a low heat and let the potatoes boil *gently* until they are soft. This should take about 15–20 minutes.

6 Test to see if the potatoes are cooked by piercing them with a fork. If the potatoes feel soft inside, then turn off the cooker.

7 Very carefully carry the saucepan of potatoes to the sink. Hold the colander over the mixing bowl and empty the contents of the saucepan into the colander.

8 Tip the strained potatoes back into the saucepan and lightly toss the potatoes over a low heat.

9 Turn off the heat and add 25 g margarine and a little chopped parsley to the saucepan. Toss the potatoes until they are evenly coated in melted fat and parsley.

10 Empty the hot potatoes into the warmed serving dish and serve immediately. (The strained potato water can be used when making the gravy. It will add flavour and goodness.)

Menu

Dinner

— ❋ —

Fried liver and onions
Boiled potatoes
Spring cabbage
Gravy

Baked stuffed apples
Custard

Chipped Potatoes

Serves 4

Ingredients needed
4 large
or 6 medium-sized potatoes
1½ kg fat or 10 dl oil

Equipment needed
1 deep frying pan
  with basket and lid
1 vegetable knife
1 plate
1 chopping board
1 mixing bowl
1 tea towel

Serving dish needed
1 vegetable dish
or a 10 dl casserole dish

Preparations
1. Collect the equipment.
2. Wash your hands.
3. Half fill a mixing bowl with cold water.
4. Peel and wash the potatoes as in recipe 11. Put each rinsed potato in the mixing bowl of cold water.
5. Put the serving dish in a warm place.

Method
1. Remove the basket from the frying pan.
2. Melt the fat in the pan over a moderate heat. Do not walk away and **forget** it.
3. While the fat is melting, cut the potatoes into slices about 1 cm width.
4. Cut the slices into thin strips or 'chips'.
5. Pat the chips dry in a clean tea towel and then tip them into the frying basket.
6. When a faint blue haze begins to rise from the fat, gently lower the basket of chips into the hot fat.
7. Cover the chip pan with a lid.
8. Cook the chips until they are soft when pierced with a vegetable knife.
9. Lift the basket of chips out of the fat.
10. Continue to heat the fat for a further minute and then plunge the chips back into the pan. This second cooking will brown and crisp the chips.
11. When a golden brown in colour, remove the basket and allow the chips to drain before tipping them into the warmed dish. Turn off the cooker.

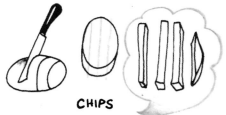

CHIPS

BASKET OF CHIPS READY TO BE FRIED

Menu

Lunch

— ✳ —

Steak and kidney pie
Chipped potatoes
Brussels sprouts
Gravy

Semolina pudding

 **Grilled Tomatoes** *Serves 4*

Ingredients needed
8 tomatoes
25 g margarine
salt and pepper
sprig of parsley

Equipment needed
1 chopping board
1 vegetable knife
1 sheet of foil (about
    23 cm × 15 cm)
1 grill pan

Serving dish needed
1 oval plate
or 1 casserole lid

Preparations
1 Collect the equipment.
2 Turn on the grill.
3 Line the grill pan with aluminium foil.
4 Wash your hands.
5 Wash the tomatoes or wipe them with a clean, damp cloth.
6 Chop parsley.

Method
1 Cut the tomatoes in half across the 'equator'.
2 Place the halves of tomatoes, cut side upwards, in the bottom of the grill pan.
3 Sprinkle the tomatoes with salt and pepper.
4 Put a small piece of margarine on the top of each half of tomato.
5 Grill the tomatoes for 5 minutes. Test to see if the insides are soft by piercing them with a fork.
6 Sprinkle the tomatoes with freshly-chopped parsley and serve them on a warmed plate.
7 This dish can be garnished with slices of lemon and a green vegetable.

Menu

Lunch
— ✳ —
Russian fish pie
Grilled tomatoes
Peas
Parsley sauce

Banana custard

 # Boiled 'Frozen' Vegetables

Serves 4

Ingredients needed

*1 large packet of frozen
    vegetables*
or *2 small packets*
500 ml water
$\frac{1}{4} \times$ 5 ml spoon salt
25 g margarine
sprig of mint

Equipment needed

1 saucepan
a 5 ml spoon
1 measure

Serving dish needed

1 vegetable dish
or *a 10 dl casserole dish*

Preparations

1 Collect the equipment.
2 Wash your hands.
3 Put the serving dish in a warm place.

Method

1 Put 500 ml cold water into a saucepan. Add $\frac{1}{4} \times$ 5 ml spoon salt and a sprig of mint. (If cooking frozen peas, also add $\frac{1}{2} \times$ 5 ml spoon sugar. This will improve the flavour.)
2 Place the lid on the saucepan and quickly bring the water to the boil.
3 Turn the heat low and add the frozen vegetables. Replace the lid. Cook the vegetables in the gently boiling water for 5–8 minutes.
4 When the vegetables are cooked, carefully strain the liquid into a basin.
5 Put 25 g margarine into the saucepan and toss the strained, cooked vegetables until the fat has melted.
6 Tip the vegetables into the warmed dish and serve immediately.

Menu

Dinner

— ✳ —

Grilled pork chop
Apple sauce
Boiled potatoes
Green beans (frozen)
Gravy

Pineapple
upside-down pudding
Custard

 **Boiled 'Fresh' Green Vegetables** *Serves 4*

Ingredients needed
1 kg cabbage
or 1 kg brussels sprouts
or 1 kg peas
or 1 kg runner beans
1 × 5 ml spoon salt
25 g margarine
500 ml water

Equipment needed
1 vegetable knife
1 chopping board
1 saucepan with lid

Serving dish needed
1 vegetable dish
or a 10 dl casserole dish

Preparations
1 Collect the equipment.
2 Wash your hands.
3 Collect the ingredients.
4 Put the serving dish in a warm place.
5 Prepare the vegetables for cooking:

Cabbage	Remove and throw away the withered outer leaves. Separate the leaves and put them to soak in cold water with 2 × 5 ml spoons salt ($\frac{1}{4}$ hr.)	Rinse well	Cut out the tough stalk from each leaf	Chop the leaves into strips
Brussels sprouts	Remove outer withered leaves and throw away. Make a cross cut (X) at the bottom of each sprout. Leave to soak in cold water with 2 × 5 ml spoons salt ($\frac{1}{4}$ hr.)			Rinse well
Peas	Shell Rinse well			
Runner beans	With a knife, remove the thread from the 'long' side of each bean	Rinse well	Cut the beans into short strips about 5 cm long	

Method
1 Place 500 ml water and 1 × 5 ml spoon salt in a saucepan. Boil.
2 When boiling, add the prepared vegetables. Cover the saucepan with a lid. Continue boiling until the vegetables are cooked (15 minutes).
3 Strain well. (The cooking liquid can be used for the gravy.)
4 Add 25 g margarine and toss the vegetables lightly until they are evenly-coated in melted fat.
5 Empty into the warmed serving dish. Serve at once.

Dinner
— ❋ —
Meat and potato pie
Green beans
Gravy

Fresh peaches
Coffee

Gravy

Serves 4

(Blending method)

Ingredients needed
500 ml vegetable water
25 g plain flour
1 × 5 ml spoon gravy powder
  (e.g. Bisto)
pinch of salt
sprinkle of pepper
1 oxo cube (if liked)

Equipment needed
1 small saucepan
1 wooden spoon
a 5 dl basin
a 5 ml spoon
a 20 ml spoon

Serving dish needed
a 5 dl sauceboat
or *jug*

Preparations
1 Collect the equipment
2 Wash your hands.
3 Strain 500 ml of cooking liquid from any vegetable being boiled.

Method
1 Place the flour and gravy powder into a small basin. Add 20 ml cold water and stir to form a smooth paste.
2 Gradually stir in the 500 ml vegetable water. Season with salt and pepper.
3 A crumbled oxo cube can be added, if liked.
4 Pour the liquid into a saucepan and cook over a low heat, stirring well with a wooden spoon.
5 When the gravy has thickened, cook for a further 2 minutes. Taste. If necessary, add more seasoning.
6 If a joint has been roasted, 1 × 20 ml spoon of the meat sediment and fat which collects at the bottom of the roasting tin will add flavour and goodness to a gravy.
7 If vegetable water is not available use a beef stock cube, or even cold water and a meat extract (e.g. marmite).
8 Pour the gravy into the sauceboat or jug and serve while hot.

Dinner

— ❋ —

Roast fillet of lamb
Baked potatoes
Buttered parsnips
Gravy

Gooseberry sponge
Custard

 **White Sauce**   Serves 4

Ingredients needed

500 ml milk
50 g margarine
50 g plain flour
$\frac{1}{4} \times 5$ ml spoon salt
pepper

Flavourings

50 g grated cheese
2 chopped hard-boiled eggs
3 × 5 ml spoons chopped
  parsley
2 × 5 ml spoons grated
  raw onion
3 × 5 ml spoons sugar

Equipment needed

1 medium-sized saucepan
1 wooden spoon
1 pan stand
or formica mat
1 plate
1 measure
a 5 ml spoon

Serving dish

a 5 dl sauceboat
or jug

Preparations

1 Collect the equipment.
2 Wash your hands.
3 Weigh the ingredients.
4 Prepare the flavouring, i.e. grate the cheese; chop the parsley, onion or egg.

Method

1 Put the margarine in the saucepan.
2 Melt the fat over a low heat. Do not let the margarine get too hot or 'sizzle'.
3 Place the saucepan on a pan stand and stir the flour into the melted fat, using a wooden spoon. The dry paste which is formed is called a **roux.**
4 Return the saucepan to the low heat and cook the roux for 2 minutes, stirring all the time. Return the saucepan to the pan stand.
5 Add the milk to the cooked roux, **a drop at a time.** After each drop of milk, stir the roux vigorously to keep it smooth and free from lumps.
6 When all the milk has been added, season the sauce with salt and pepper (**not** if you are making a sweet sauce).
7 Return the saucepan to the low heat and gently bring the sauce to the boil. Stir all the time to prevent the sauce from becoming lumpy.

8 When the sauce has thickened, cook it for a further 2 minutes and then turn off the heat.

9 Add any of the suggested flavourings to the sauce. If using sugar to make a sweet sauce omit the salt and pepper.

10 Taste the sauce.

11 If necessary, add more seasoning or flavouring.

12 Serve the sauce while it is hot. If you must keep it warm for any length of time, cover the saucepan with a clean, damp cloth and fasten the lid firmly on the saucepan. This will prevent the sauce from forming a skin. When the sauce is needed, re-heat it, stirring all the time.

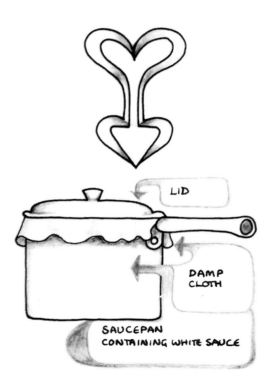

LID

DAMP CLOTH

SAUCEPAN CONTAINING WHITE SAUCE

Menu

(with savoury white sauce)

Dinner

— ✳ —

Cold brisket of beef
Chipped potatoes

Cauliflower
and baby beetroot
in onion sauce

Pear melba

Menu

(with a sweet white sauce)

Dinner

— ✳ —

Roast lamb
Mint sauce
Jacket potatoes
Brussels sprouts
Gravy

Treacle pudding
White sauce

Mint Sauce

Serves 4

Ingredients needed
4 sprigs of mint
1 × 5 ml spoon sugar
125 ml vinegar

Equipment needed
1 mint chopper
or 1 sharp knife
1 chopping board
a 5 ml spoon
1 measure

Serving dish needed
1 sauceboat
or jug

LEAVES

Preparations
1 Collect the equipment.
2 Wash your hands.
3 Collect the ingredients.
4 Wash the mint.
5 Pull the leaves from the sprigs of mint and place them on a chopping board.

Method
1 Using either a mint chopper or a sharp knife, chop the leaves of mint finely.
2 Place the chopped mint in a sauceboat and add sugar.
3 Pour 125 ml vinegar on to the mint and sugar, and stir well.

Remember that the flavour of mint sauce goes well with lamb but there is no reason why you should not serve it with other meats.

Menu

Dinner

— ✳ —

Grilled lamb chop
Mint sauce
Boiled potatoes
Carrots
Gravy

Baked apples
Custard

Rice Pudding

Serves 4

Ingredients needed
500 ml milk
50 g rice
25 g sugar
a nutmeg

Equipment needed
1 sieve
1 grater
a 20 ml spoon
1 measure

Serving dish needed
a 10 dl ovenproof dish

Preparations
1 Collect the equipment.
2 Heat the oven at gas mark 3 or 170°C.
3 Grease the ovenproof dish.
4 Wash your hands.
5 Wash the rice in a sieve.

Method
1 Put the washed rice in the bottom of the greased oven-proof dish.
2 Add the sugar.
3 Pour the milk over the rice and sugar and stir all the ingredients together.
4 Grate a little nutmeg on the top of the pudding.
5 Cook the rice pudding in the middle of the oven for 2 hours.
6 This dish can be served hot or cold.

Menu
Dinner
— ❋ —
Scotch eggs
Creamed potatoes
Green salad

Rice pudding

20 Bread and Butter Pudding

Serves 4

Ingredients needed

4 large slices bread
50 g butter
500 ml milk
2 eggs
50 g sugar
25 g currants

Equipment needed

1 round-bladed knife
1 measure
1 fork
1 basin
1 sieve
a 20 ml spoon

Serving dish needed

a 10 dl ovenproof dish

Preparations

1 Collect the equipment.
2 Heat the oven at gas mark 3 or 170°C.
3 Grease the ovenproof dish.
4 Wash the currants in a sieve.
5 Butter the slices of bread and cut them into fingers.

Method

1 Place half of the buttered fingers of bread in an ovenproof dish.
2 Scatter half of the cleaned currants on the bread.
3 Put the remaining fingers of bread on top and add the rest of the currants.
4 Break the eggs in a basin and beat them lightly with a fork.
5 Stir in the sugar.
6 Carefully add 500 ml milk and stir well.
7 Pour the custard mixture over the bread, butter and currants.
8 Leave the pudding for ½ hour before baking.
9 Bake the pudding in the middle of the oven for 30–40 minutes until the custard is set and the bread crisp and brown.
10 This pudding can be served by itself, or it can be served with a custard powder sauce.

Menu

Dinner

— ❋ —

Grilled plaice with lemon
Baked potatoes
Garden peas
Parsley sauce

Bread and butter pudding

Apple Crumble

Serves 4

Ingredients needed
150 g plain flour
75 g margarine
125 g sugar
500 g baking apples

Equipment needed
1 mixing bowl
1 round-bladed knife
1 vegetable knife
1 plate
a 20 ml spoon

Serving dish needed
a 10 dl ovenproof dish

Preparations
1 Collect the equipment.
2 Heat the oven at gas mark 4 or 180°C.
3 Wash your hands.
4 Weigh the ingredients.

Method
1 Using your fingertips, rub the margarine into the flour until the mixture looks like fine breadcrumbs.
2 Add 75 g sugar and stir it in well.
3 Peel and wash the apples. Cut them into quarters and slice each quarter into thin pieces.
4 Place half of the sliced apple into the ovenproof dish.
5 Sprinkle 50 g sugar over the apple.
6 Place the rest of the apple on top.
7 Cover the apple with the cake mixture.
8 Bake the apple crumble in the middle of the oven for 35 minutes.
9 This dish can be served hot with a custard sauce or eaten when cold with cream or evaporated milk.

Menu

Dinner
— ❋ —
Grilled sausages
Mashed potatoes
Brussels sprouts
Gravy

Apple crumble
Custard

Steamed Jam Sponge

Serves 4

Ingredients needed
50 g margarine
50 g sugar
1 egg
75 g S.R. flour
1 × 20 ml spoon jam

Equipment needed
1 piece greaseproof paper
1 piece string
1 small basin
1 fork
1 wooden spoon
1 mixing bowl
1 sieve
1 large saucepan
1 steamer with lid
a 20 ml spoon
a 5 dl pudding basin

Serving dish needed
1 large plate

Preparations
1 Collect the equipment.
2 Half fill a large saucepan with cold water and place over a low heat.
3 Grease the pudding basin and sheet of greaseproof paper.
4 Wash your hands.
5 Weigh the ingredients.

Method
1 Place the jam in the bottom of the greased basin.
2 Using a wooden spoon, cream the fat and sugar in a mixing bowl, until they become white and fluffy.
3 Break the egg into a small basin and beat it lightly with a fork.
4 Add the beaten egg to the creamed fat and sugar a drop at a time. Beat the mixture well.
5 Add about ⅓ of the sieved flour and fold it into the mixture carefully using a metal spoon. Fold in the remaining flour a third at a time.
6 Place the cake mixture on top of the jam in the greased basin. Cover it with the sheet of greaseproof paper. Fasten the paper onto the basin with string.

A LID OF GREASEPROOF PAPER TIED ON WITH STRING

7   Place the pudding inside the steamer and cover with a tightly-fitting lid.

8   Carefully pull the saucepan of boiling water off the heat and place the steamer on top. Return the saucepan to the heat and steam the pudding for $1\frac{1}{2}$ hours. (Check every $\frac{1}{2}$ hour to see that the saucepan still contains plenty of water. If necessary, add more **hot** water to the saucepan to prevent it from boiling dry.)

9   After $1\frac{1}{2}$ hours, carefully remove the steamer from the saucepan and take out the hot basin. Use **oven gloves.**

10   Untie the string and peel the paper back.

11   Slide a knife around the inside of the dish to loosen the pudding.

12   Place a warmed plate over the basin and very carefully tip the basin upside down. Remove the basin and the pudding should slip out onto the plate.

13   Serve the steamed pudding while hot, with a sweet white sauce or with a custard.

Menu

Dinner

— ❋ —

Curried eggs
Shredded raw cabbage
Sliced tomatoes

Jam sponge
White sauce

STEAMER ON SAUCEPAN OF BOILING WATER

PLATE

Fruit Pie

Serves 4

Ingredients needed
100 g plain flour
¼ × 5 ml spoon salt
25 g margarine
25 g lard
20 ml cold water

Filling
1 tin of either
　damsons
　gooseberries
　stewed apples
　bilberries
　rhubarb

Equipment needed
1 mixing bowl
1 round-bladed knife
1 rolling pin
1 flour dredger
1 small basin
1 fork
1 tin opener
1 vegetable knife
a 20 ml spoon

Serving dish needed
1 shallow ovenproof dish
　(must not be deeper than 5 cm)

5cm

Preparations
1 Collect the equipment.
2 Heat the oven at gas mark 7 or 220°C.
3 Wash your hands.
4 Weigh the ingredients.
5 Open the tin of fruit.

Method
1 Prepare the pastry:
a Sieve the flour and salt together into a mixing bowl.
b Using the fingertips, rub the fat into the flour, until the
　 mixture resembles fine breadcrumbs.
c Add 20 ml cold water and stir well with a round-bladed
　 knife.
d Squeeze or knead the pastry together with one hand.
　 The pastry should be dry but not too crumbly.
2 Place the fruit in the bottom of the ovenproof dish and half
　cover it with the syrup from the tin.

LEVEL OF SYRUP

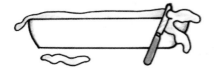

3 Roll out the pastry on a lightly-floured board until it is just bigger than the top of the dish.

4 Lift the pastry on top of the dish and press firmly around the edge.

5 Trim the extra pastry off neatly, using a knife.

6 Decorate the edge of the pie by pressing down with the blade of a vegetable knife or the prongs of a fork.

7 Prick the pastry two or three times to allow the steam to escape when the pie is cooking.

8 Bake the pie at the top of the oven for 20–30 minutes.

9 When cooked, sprinkle the pie with castor sugar.

10 Either serve the pie hot with a custard sauce or cold with cream or evaporated milk.

Menu

Dinner

— ✳ —

Shepherd's pie
Spinach
Gravy

Fruit pie
Custard sauce

Egg Salad

Serves 4

Ingredients needed
4 eggs
2 tomatoes
¼ cucumber
a small lettuce
50 g grated cheese
1 orange
bunch of radishes

Equipment needed
1 plate
1 vegetable knife
1 chopping board
1 colander
1 small saucepan
1 grater
a 20 ml spoon

Serving dish needed
1 large oval
or round plate

Preparations
1 Collect the equipment.
2 Wash your hands.
3 Prepare the eggs:
a Half fill the saucepan with cold water and put it on the cooker at full heat.
b When the water has reached boiling point, turn the heat very **low** and allow the water to simmer gently. Lower the eggs into the saucepan.
c Cook the eggs in simmering water for 10 minutes.
d Immediately after 10 minutes turn off the heat and cool the hard-boiled eggs quickly in cold water.
4 While the eggs are cooking, wash the lettuce leaves in running water. Place them in a colander and shake until the leaves are almost dry.
5 Wipe the tomatoes with a damp cloth.
6 Peel the cucumber thinly.
7 Grate the cheese.
8 Peel the orange.
9 Remove the top and tail of each radish and then wash the radishes in the colander.
Now you are ready to make the salad.

WASHED LETTUCE LEAVES AND RADISH IN COLANDER

WIPED TOMATOES

PEELED ORANGE

PEELED CUCUMBER

GRATED CHEESE

CUT HERE

4 QUARTERS OF TOMATO

SOUTH POLE

NORTH POLE

SLICES OF ORANGE

CUT HERE

CUT HERE

CUT HERE

Method

1 Cut the tomatoes into quarters.
2 Cut the orange into slices.
3 Cut the cucumber into thin slices.
4 Shell the eggs and cut each one into halves.
5 Arrange the lettuce leaves neatly on a plate.
6 Carefully place the rest of the ingredients on the lettuce. Try to have a simple pattern in mind and do not make the salad look too 'fussy'. Below are two examples of how these salad ingredients can be arranged attractively.
7 Egg salad should be served with salad cream or mayonnaise.

Menu

High Tea
— ✳ —
Egg salad
Bread and butter

Fruit flan
Cream

Chocolate cake
Tea

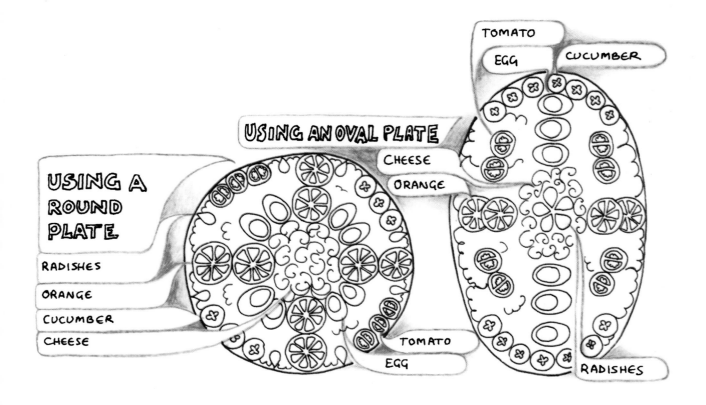

USING A ROUND PLATE

RADISHES
ORANGE
CUCUMBER
CHEESE

USING AN OVAL PLATE

CHEESE
ORANGE
TOMATO
EGG

TOMATO
EGG
CUCUMBER
RADISHES

Stuffed Cheese Potatoes

Serves 4

Ingredients needed
4 medium-sized potatoes
100 g grated cheese
1 tomato
sprig of parsley
25 g margarine
20 ml milk

Equipment needed
1 baking sheet
1 sheet aluminium foil
1 fork
1 vegetable knife
1 grater
1 plate
1 basin
a 20 ml spoon

Serving dish needed
1 large oval
or *round plate*

Preparations
1 Collect the equipment.
2 Heat the oven at gas mark 6 or 200°C.
3 Line the baking sheet with aluminium foil.
4 Wash your hands.
5 Scrub the potatoes well under running cold water. Pat them dry on a clean cloth. Prick each potato four times with a fork before placing it on the baking sheet.
6 Bake the potatoes until they are soft when pierced with a fork. (The length of cooking time will depend upon the size of the potato. Try 1 hour for a medium-sized potato.)
7 Grate the cheese.
8 Put the serving dish in a warm place.

Method
1 Cut each cooked potato in half lengthways.
2 Scoop out the centre of each potato with a teaspoon, placing the cooked potato in a basin.
3 Mash the cooked potato with a fork.
4 Add 25 g margarine and 20 ml milk to the mashed potato, and beat the mixture well until it turns creamy.
5 Stir 75 g grated cheese into the creamed potato.

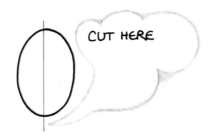

CUT HERE

6 Divide the cheese and potato mixture amongst the potato cases.

7 Sprinkle the remaining 25 g cheese over the potato cases.

8 Replace the stuffed potatoes carefully onto the baking sheet and return them to the oven for ½ hour. The stuffed potatoes may be browned under a hot grill for 5 minutes instead of returning them to the oven.

9 Place the browned cheese potatoes onto a warmed plate and decorate them with slices of tomato and a sprig of parsley.

Menu

Supper

— ❋ —

Stuffed cheese potatoes
Celery

Glass of milk

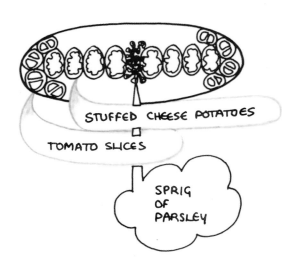

STUFFED CHEESE POTATOES

TOMATO SLICES

SPRIG OF PARSLEY

Cornish Pasties

Serves 4

Ingredients needed
100 g plain flour
$\frac{1}{4}$ × 5 ml spoon salt
25 g margarine
25 g lard
20 ml cold water
100 g minced beef
1 small onion
1 small carrot
salt and pepper
1 egg

Equipment needed
1 mixing bowl
1 round-bladed knife
1 rolling pin
1 flour dredger
1 plain 15 cm pastry cutter
or 1 saucer
1 grater
1 plate
a 20 ml spoon
a 5 ml spoon
1 pastry brush
1 sieve
1 small basin
1 baking sheet

Serving dish needed
1 large oval
or round plate

Preparations
1 Collect the equipment.
2 Heat the oven at gas mark 7 or 220°C.
3 Wash your hands.
4 Weigh the ingredients.
5 Peel and rinse the carrot.
6 Remove the skin from the onion.

Method
1 Prepare the pastry:
a Sieve the flour and salt together into a mixing bowl.
b Using the fingertips, rub the fat into the flour, until the mixture resembles fine breadcrumbs.
c Add 20 ml cold water and stir well with a round-bladed knife.
d Squeeze (knead) the pastry together with one hand. The pastry should be dry but not crumbly.

Menu

High Tea

— ✳ —

Cornish pasties
Green salad
Chutney
Bread and butter

Fruit in jelly
Blancmange

Tea

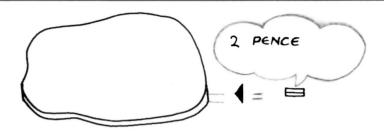

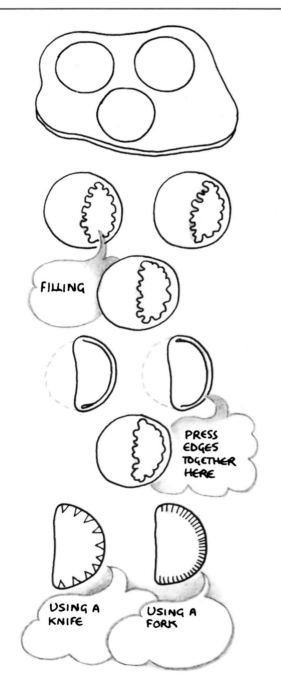

2 Prepare the filling:
a Empty the minced beef onto a plate.
b Grate the carrot and onion onto the minced beef.
c Stir the filling well and season with $\frac{1}{4} \times 5$ ml spoon salt and a dash of pepper.
3 Roll out the pastry on a lightly-floured board until it is the thickness of 2 new pennies.
4 Stamp out 3 circles using a pastry cutter (or cut round a saucer).
5 Place the circles of pastry to one side and squeeze the remaining pieces of pastry together.
6 Roll out the rest of the pastry and cut out 1 more circle of pastry.
7 Place the 4 pastry circles side by side and divide the filling amongst them.
8 Dampen a pastry brush in cold water and wipe round each circle of pastry.
9 Fold the pastry circles over and press the edges together firmly.
10 Decorate the edges of each pasty using a vegetable knife or a fork.
11 Place the pasties on a baking sheet.
12 Prick each pasty with a fork. These holes will let any steam escape during cooking.
13 Brush over each pasty with a little beaten egg.
14 Bake the pasties for $\frac{1}{2}$ hour. (After 15 minutes turn the oven down to gas mark 4 or 180°C.)
15 Cornish pasties can be served hot with potatoes or cold with a salad and pickles.

Sausage Rolls

Serves 4

Ingredients
1 small packet frozen
  flaky pastry
200 g sausagemeat
1 egg

Equipment needed
1 baking sheet
1 round-bladed knife
1 rolling pin
1 flour dredger
1 pastry brush
1 small basin
1 fork

Serving dish
1 large oval
or round plate

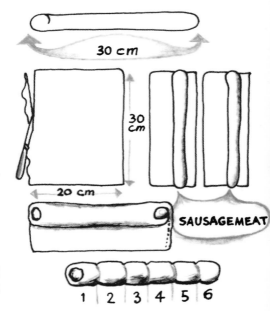

SAUSAGEMEAT

Preparations
1 Unwrap the pastry and allow it to thaw gently before using.
2 Collect the equipment.
3 Heat the oven at gas mark 7 or 220°C.
4 Wash your hands.
5 Collect the remaining ingredients.
6 Break the egg into a basin and beat it lightly with a fork.
7 Divide the sausagemeat into two equal pieces. Using floured hands shape each portion of sausagemeat into a long roll about 30 cm long.

Method
1 Roll the pastry into a long strip, about 30 cm × 20 cm. Trim the sides straight with a knife.
2 Cut down the centre of the pastry to form two long, thin pieces of pastry.
3 Place each strip of sausagemeat on a strip of pastry.
4 With cold water and a pastry brush, brush down each side of pastry.
5 Roll each strip of pastry around the sausagemeat.
6 Brush down the length of each sausage roll with beaten egg and then cut each strip into 6 pieces.
7 Place the 12 sausage rolls on a baking sheet and prick each one with a fork.
8 Bake in a hot oven for 30 minutes.
9 Sausage rolls can be served hot, or cold with a salad.

Menu

High Tea

— ❋ —

Sausage rolls
Green salad
Bread and butter

Stewed damsons
Cream

Tea

Egg Mayonnaise

Serves 4

Ingredients needed

4 slices of bread
50 g butter
4 eggs
I small bottle of
  salad cream
10 ml vinegar
salt and pepper
sprig of parsley
I tomato

Equipment needed

I bread board
I round-bladed knife
I saucepan
I egg slice
I small basin
a 10 ml spoon

Serving dish needed

I large oval
or round plate

Preparations

1 Collect the equipment.
2 Wash your hands.
3 Collect the ingredients.
4 Cook the eggs in simmering water for 10 minutes. When hard-boiled, cool the eggs quickly in cold water.
5 Butter each slice of bread.

Method

1 Shell the cold hard-boiled eggs and cut them into thin slices using an egg slicer or knife.
2 Arrange a sliced egg over each piece of buttered bread, and lightly sprinkle with salt and pepper.
3 Empty the small bottle of salad cream into a basin and add 10 ml vinegar. Stir.
4 Using a spoon, coat the slices of egg with salad cream.
5 Decorate each egg mayonnaise with a slice of tomato and a sprig of parsley.

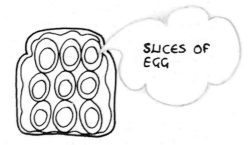

SLICES OF EGG

SPRIG OF PARSLEY

HALF SLICES OF TOMATO

Menu

Supper

— ❈ —

Egg mayonnaise

An apple
Glass of milk

Banana Custard

Serves 4

Ingredients needed
4 bananas
500 ml milk
2 × 20 ml spoons custard
    powder
2 × 20 ml spoons sugar
coconut or chocolate flakes

Equipment needed
1 medium saucepan
1 wooden spoon
1 chopping board
1 vegetable knife
a 20 ml spoon
1 measure

Serving dish needed
1 large fruit dish
or 4 small fruit dishes

Preparations
1 Collect the equipment.
2 Wash your hands.
3 Measure the ingredients.

Method
1 Place the custard powder and sugar in the saucepan.
2 Add 20 ml milk and mix the custard powder and sugar to a smooth paste, stirring with a wooden spoon.
3 Gradually stir in the remaining milk.
4 Heat the custard over a low heat, stirring all the time.
5 As the mixture starts to boil, the custard will thicken.
6 Cook for a further 2 minutes.
7 Leave the saucepan of custard in a cold place to cool. Stir every few minutes.
8 When the custard is cool, peel the bananas and slice them thinly into the serving dish.
9 Pour the custard over the bananas.
10 Decorate the dish with coconut or flakes of chocolate.

Menu

High Tea

— ✳ —

Boiled ham
Green salad
Bread and butter

Banana custard

Tea

Trifle

Serves 4

Ingredients needed
½ *Swiss roll (jam)*
I tall tin fruit
250 ml milk
I × 20 ml spoon custard
   powder
I × 20 ml spoon sugar
I tin cream
chocolate flakes
20 ml sherry (if liked)

Equipment needed
I saucepan
I wooden spoon
I tin opener
I small basin
I round-bladed knife
I sieve
I fork
a 20 ml spoon
I measure

Serving dish needed
a 10 dl fruit dish
or *casserole dish*

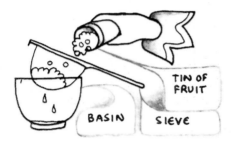

TIN OF
FRUIT

BASIN   SIEVE

Preparations
1 Collect the equipment.
2 Wash your hands.
3 Collect the ingredients.
4 Open the tin of fruit and strain off the syrup.
5 Cut the ½ Swiss roll into thin slices and place in the serving dish.

Method
1 Sprinkle 4 × 20 ml spoons fruit syrup over the cake. A 20 ml spoon sherry may be added, if liked.
2 Place the strained fruit on the top of the cake.
3 Make 250 ml custard sauce (see recipe 29) and when cool, pour the custard over the fruit. Leave to set.
4 Empty the tin of cream into a basin and whip lightly with a fork.
5 Spread the cream evenly over the layer of custard.
6 Decorate the trifle with chocolate flakes.

Menu

High Tea
— ✳ —
Crab salad
Bread and butter

Trifle

Cakes
Tea

Blancmange

Serves 4

Ingredients needed
500 ml milk
1 pkt blancmange powder
50 g sugar
coconut

Equipment needed
1 saucepan
1 wooden spoon
a 5 dl mould
1 measure

Serving dish needed
1 large fruit dish
or large plate

Preparations
1 Collect the equipment.
2 Wash your hands.
3 Collect the ingredients.
4 If a mould is being used, fill the mould with cold water and leave it to stand until needed.

Method
1 Empty the packet of blancmange powder and the sugar into the saucepan.
2 Add a drop of milk at a time, and stir well with a wooden spoon.
3 When the powder and sugar has been blended to a smooth paste, the remaining milk can be gradually stirred in.
4 Cook the blancmange over a low heat, stirring all the time.
5 As the mixture starts to boil, the blancmange will thicken.
6 Cook for a further 2 minutes.
7 If a glass dish is being used, let the blancmange cool slightly before being poured in. Decorate with coconut, when set.
8 If a mould is being used, empty the water before quickly pouring in the blancmange. Leave to set.
9 When the blancmange has set in the mould, ease the blancmange from the sides of the mould, using your fingers.
10 Put the large plate over the mould and turn upside down. After a few shakes, the mould can be lifted off carefully, leaving the blancmange on the plate.

Menu

High Tea

— ✳ —

Tongue salad
Bread and butter
Celery

Blancmange
Cream

Tea

Fruit Salad

Serves 4

Ingredients
2 *eating apples*
2 *oranges*
2 *bananas*
small tin cherries
100 g sugar

Equipment needed
1 vegetable knife
1 plate
1 chopping board
1 saucepan
1 wooden spoon
1 tin opener
1 measure

Serving dish
a 10 dl casserole
or fruit dish

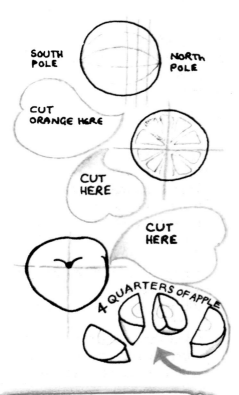

SOUTH POLE

NORTH POLE

CUT ORANGE HERE

CUT HERE

CUT HERE

4 QUARTERS OF APPLE

Preparations
1 Collect the equipment.
2 Wash your hands.
3 Collect the ingredients.
4 Open the tin of fruit and pour the syrup into a measure. Add cold water to make the liquid up to 250 ml.
5 Place the 250 ml of liquid into the saucepan and add the sugar.
6 Heat gently and stir with a wooden spoon until the sugar has dissolved.
7 Allow the liquid to boil vigorously for 5 minutes. This will form a syrup in which to serve the fruit.
8 While the syrup is cooling, peel the oranges.
9 Cut the tinned cherries in half and remove the stones.

Method
1 Pour the cool syrup into the serving dish. Add the cherries.
2 Cut the oranges into thin slices, parallel with the 'equator'.
3 Cut each slice of orange into quarters.
4 Place the small pieces of orange into the syrup.
5 Peel the apples thinly.
6 Cut the apples into quarters and remove the centres with the pips.
7 Cut each quarter into segments and add to the syrup.
8 Skin the bananas and cut into rings. Add to the syrup.
9 Stir all the fruit together before serving with cream, ice-cream or evaporated milk.

Menu

High Tea

— ✳ —

Eggs in cheese sauce
Bread and butter

Fruit salad
Cream

Fruit loaf
Tea

 **Fruit in Jelly** **Serves 4**

Ingredients needed
1 jelly
1 tin of fruit

Equipment needed
1 kettle
1 tin opener
1 basin
1 sieve
1 pair kitchen scissors
1 measure
a 20 ml spoon

Serving dish needed
a large fruit dish
or 4 individual fruit dishes

Preparations
1 Collect the equipment.
2 Wash your hands.
3 Collect the ingredients.
4 Open the tin of fruit and strain off the syrup into a basin.
5 Cut the jelly into quarters and place in the measure.
6 Half fill the kettle with cold water and bring to the boil.

Method
1 Pour 125 ml boiling water over the jelly cubes. Stir well until the jelly cubes are dissolved.
2 Add the cold fruit juice to the 125 ml jelly, and then make up the quantity to 500 ml with cold water. Stir well.
3 Pour the jelly into the serving dish and leave in a cool place.
4 After 1 hour, add the strained fruit and stir in gently. Leave to set. Fruit in jelly can be served with blancmange, ice-cream or cream.

Menu

High Tea
— ❋ —
Egg, cheese and
tomato flan
Chipped potatoes
Green salad

Fruit in jelly
Evaporated milk

Tea

 **Shortbread Biscuits** *Makes 10*

Ingredients needed
150 g plain flour
100 g butter or margarine
50 g sugar
12 g caster sugar
  (for decoration)

Equipment needed
1 mixing bowl
1 round-bladed knife
1 fork
1 rolling pin
1 flour dredger
1 fancy pastry cutter
1 baking sheet
1 cooling tray
a 20 ml spoon

Serving dish needed
1 medium-sized plate with
  d'oyley

Preparations
1 Collect the equipment.
2 Heat the oven at gas mark 5 or 190°C.
3 Wash your hands.
4 Weigh the ingredients.
5 Sprinkle flour over the baking sheet.

Method
1 Using the fingertips, rub the fat into the flour until the mixture looks like fine breadcrumbs.
2 Add the sugar and stir in well.
3 Using one hand, knead or squeeze the mixture until it becomes like soft pastry.
4 Roll out the shortbread mixture until it is 1 cm thick.
5 Using a fancy pastry cutter stamp out as many biscuits as possible. Place them carefully on the floured baking sheet. Any mixture left over can be kneaded together, rolled and cut to make extra biscuits.
6 Prick each biscuit two or three times with a fork. This adds a decoration and keeps the biscuits flat during cooking.
7 Bake the shortbread biscuits in the middle of the oven until they are golden brown in colour (about 20 minutes).
8 When cooked, sprinkle the biscuits with caster sugar and lift them carefully on to a wire tray to cool.

Menu

Afternoon Tea
— ❋ —

Salmon and cucumber
sandwiches
Fruit scones
Shortbread biscuits
Buttered malt loaf
Tea

Rock Buns

Makes 8

Ingredients needed
100 g S.R. flour
50 g margarine
50 g sugar
50 g currants
$\frac{1}{4}$ × 5 ml spoon salt
$\frac{1}{2}$ egg

Equipment needed
1 mixing bowl
1 round-bladed knife
1 measure
1 fork
1 baking sheet
1 sieve
a 5 ml spoon

Serving dish needed
1 medium-sized plate with d'oyley

Preparations
1 Collect the equipment.
2 Heat the oven at gas mark 7 or 220°C.
3 Wash your hands.
4 Weigh the ingredients.
5 Wash the currants in a sieve (see diagram page 166).
6 Flour the baking sheet.

Method
1 Sieve the flour and salt together.
2 Using the fingertips, rub the fat into the flour.
3 Add the sugar and washed currants. Stir in.
4 Break the egg into a measure and beat well with a fork.
5 Add the beaten egg to the mixture, a drop at a time, pressing in firmly with a knife. A **stiff** dough should be formed.
6 Place the mixture on the floured baking sheet in rough 'rocky' heaps.
7 Bake the rock buns at the top of the oven for 15–20 minutes, until they are golden brown in colour and firm to the touch.
8 When cooked place the rock buns on a cooling tray.

Menu
High Tea
— ❋ —
Pilchard salad
Brown bread and butter

Apple pie
Ice cream

Rock buns
Tea

Oatmeal Scones

Makes 12

Ingredients needed

150 g S.R. flour
50 g medium oatmeal
$\frac{1}{4} \times$ 5 ml spoon salt
25 g butter or *margarine*
50 g sugar
milk to mix

Equipment needed

1 mixing bowl
1 round-bladed knife
1 rolling pin
1 flour dredger
a 20 ml spoon
a 5 ml spoon

1 baking sheet
or *girdle*
1 cooling tray
1 saucer

Serving dish needed

1 medium-sized plate with
d'oyley

Preparations

1 Collect the equipment.
2 Heat the oven at gas mark 7 or 220°C.
3 Wash your hands.
4 Weigh the ingredients.
5 Flour the baking sheet or grease the girdle.

Method

1 Sieve the flour and salt into a mixing bowl.
2 Using the fingertips, rub the fat into the flour.
3 Add the oatmeal and sugar, and stir the mixture well.
4 Add milk until the mixture forms a soft dough.
5 Roll out the dough on a lightly-floured board until it is 1 cm thick.
6 Using a saucer as a guide, cut out two circles of dough.
7 *Either* place the two circles of dough onto the floured baking sheet and, with a knife, mark each circle into 6 pieces.
   Brush the tops of the scones with milk and then bake at the top of the oven for 10–15 minutes. The scones should be well-risen and firm to the touch when baked.
   Or mark each circle into 6 pieces and fry the scones on the greased girdle for 10 minutes. Turn the scones every few minutes to prevent burning.
8 When cooked, place the scones on a cooling tray.
9 When cool, oatmeal scones can be buttered and eaten plain or with cheese, jam or black treacle.

CUT ROUND SAUCER WITH A KNIFE

TRIMMINGS

THE SECOND CIRCLE WILL BE CUT FROM THE TRIMMINGS WHICH SHOULD BE KNEADED TOGETHER AND ROLLED OUT AS BEFORE

Menu

Afternoon Tea

— ❈ —

Oatmeal scones
with cheese
and damson jam
Welsh cheese cakes
Sultana loaf
Tea

Victoria Sandwich

Serves 8

Ingredients needed
100 g margarine
100 g sugar
2 eggs
150 g S.R. flour
2 × 20 ml spoons jam
25 g caster sugar (for decoration)

Equipment needed
1 mixing bowl
1 wooden spoon
1 small basin
1 fork
1 sieve
a 20 ml spoon

2 15–18 cm
  sandwich tins
1 piece greaseproof paper

Serving dish
1 medium-sized plate
  with d'oyley

Preparations
1 Collect the equipment.
2 Heat the oven at gas mark 4 or 180°C.
3 Wash your hands.
4 Weigh the ingredients.
5 Grease the sandwich tins and place a circle of greaseproof paper in the bottom of each.

Method
1 Using a wooden spoon, cream the fat and sugar until they become white and fluffy.
2 Break the eggs into a small basin and beat them lightly with a fork.
3 Add the beaten egg to the creamed fat and sugar a drop at a time. Beat the mixture well.
4 Add $\frac{1}{3}$ of the sieved flour and fold it into the mixture carefully using a metal spoon. Fold in the remaining flour one third at a time.
5 Divide the cake mixture between the 2 sandwich tins. Smooth flat with a knife.
6 Bake in the middle of the oven for about 30 minutes. The sponges should be golden brown in colour and 'springy' to the touch.
7 When cooked, ease the cakes from the sides of the tin using a knife. Tip the cakes onto the cooling tray.
8 When cold, sandwich the 2 cakes together with jam. Sprinkle the top of the sandwich cake with caster sugar.

Menu

High Tea

— ✳ —

Cheese omelette
Bread and butter

Fresh pineapple
Cream

Victoria sandwich
Tea

 # Flapjacks or Firelighters

Makes 8

Ingredients needed
125 g porridge oats
2 × 20 ml spoons syrup
75 g sugar
75 g margarine

Equipment needed
1 saucepan
1 wooden spoon
1 round-bladed knife
a 15–18 cm sandwich tin

Serving dish needed
1 medium-sized plate with
  d'oyley

Preparations
1 Collect the equipment.
2 Heat the oven at gas mark 4 or 180°C.
3 Wash your hands.
4 Weigh the ingredients.
5 Grease the sandwich tin.

Method
1 Place the margarine, sugar and syrup in a saucepan. Gently heat the saucepan until the fat has melted and the three ingredients can be mixed together.
2 Stir the oats into the melted ingredients. Mix well.
3 Press the mixture into the greased tin and flatten with a knife.
4 Bake in the middle of the oven for approximately $\frac{1}{2}$ hour, until the biscuit mixture is golden brown in colour and firm to the touch.
5 Cut into 8 pieces with a sharp knife and leave to cool.
6 When cold, ease the biscuits carefully from the sandwich tin.

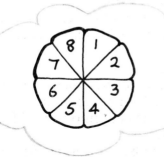

Menu

Afternoon Tea

— ✳ —

Ham in brown bread rolls
Cheese scones
Flapjacks
Swiss roll
Tea

Thomas Nelson and Sons Ltd
Nelson House   Mayfield Road
Walton-on-Thames   Surrey
KT12 5PL   UK

51 York Place
Edinburgh
EH1 3JD   UK

Thomas Nelson (Hong Kong) Ltd
Toppan Building 10/F
22A Westlands Road
Quarry Bay   Hong Kong

Thomas Nelson Australia
102 Dodds Street
South Melbourne
Victoria 3205   Australia

Nelson Canada
1120 Birchmount Road
Scarborough   Ontario
M1K 5G4   Canada

First published by Blackie and Son Ltd 1971
(under ISBN 0-216-91523-6)

This edition published by Thomas Nelson and Sons Ltd 1992

ISBN 0-17-438581-1
NPN 9 8 7 6 5 4 3

Printed in Hong Kong.